Linda R Waldon

1-

# THE KINGDOM OF HEAVEN WITHIN

# The Kingdom of Heaven Within

### Blanche Hersey Hogue

The Bookmark
Santa Clarita, California

Library of Congress Control Number: 2003103944


Hogue, Blanche Hersey.
  The Kingdom of Heaven within / Blanche Hersey Hogue.

  p.
  cm.
  ISBN 0-930227-49-2



1. Christian Science. I. Title.

BX6915.H64 2003                    289.5
                                   QBI33-1089




Published by
The Bookmark
Post Office Box 801143
Santa Clarita, California 91380

# CONTENTS

# INTRODUCTION

In those eventful years when Paul wrote letters to the early Christian Churches, he could not have known that his letters would inspire and enlighten the world for centuries to come. We do not know how many letters he wrote, but those that have survived are so filled with truth and love that they continue to illumine thought with the healing Christ.

Those who are familiar with the history of the Christian Science movement, find that the writings of the early teachers such as Mrs. Hogue, are similar to the letters of Paul. Mrs. Hogue's addresses, originally intended to educate her students in the more advanced concepts of Christian Science, are so spiritual in content that they are proving to be timeless.

In the early days of the movement, certain practitioners in the church, who were doing outstanding healing work, were chosen to be Christian Science teachers. They held one class a year, and their association of students met annually to hear an address by their teacher. These addresses were often profound works on Christian Science. Unfortunately a Church policy prohibited teachers from publishing or circulating copies of their addresses, and so few addresses from these early years have survived. Yet these few are like lights shining in the darkness. They are destined to be to Christian Science what Paul's letters have been to Christianity. Among those most valued are these four addresses by Blanche Hersey Hogue.

In 1899 Mrs. Hogue was qualified to become a Christian Science teacher. For over fifty years she held her classes and association meetings in Portland, Oregon. She taught during the most inspiring and prosperous years of the movement, when churches were filled and there were testimonies of healings comparable to those of early Christianity. From the classes of these early teachers came practitioners who did phenomenal healing work. These few addresses are an example of the dynamic teaching taking place at that time.

Often works on Christian Science tell what it teaches, but they do not explain how to demonstrate it. Mrs. Hogue' addresses reach us where we are, and she expresses her ideas in such simple language that we gain a better insight on how to heal through prayer alone.

Like Paul, she instructs, inspires, and admonishes us to give up the human for the divine. Now her addresses go beyond their original purpose. They serve to educate Christian Scientists today in the art and Science of spiritual healing. Thus, these few writings that came from her years of selfless devotion to the Cause now go forth to bless and heal in a way she could not have foreseen when she shared these addresses with her students.

A. B.

# THE KINGDOM OF HEAVEN WITHIN
## Association Address

The great objective of Christ Jesus was the kingdom, with God the Father obeyed as King. The basis and essence of all that he said and did, were concerned with the Father and the kingdom of heaven. We are still on our way to finding ourselves in that kingdom, governed by that King. The journey began when we resolved to work as Christian Scientists. We are like the merchantman with his pearl of great price, daily selling or putting off the mortal self, and buying or putting on some further portion of heaven.

### The Lord's Prayer

This kingdom is expressed in Jesus' phrase in his beloved prayer, "Thy will be done in earth, as it is in heaven," and Mary Baker Eddy's interpretation of it, ". . . as in heaven, so on earth, . . ." Jesus' prayer, the Lord's Prayer, includes all that makes heaven. (See *Science and Health With Key to the Scriptures*, page 16, for the "Lord's Prayer" and its spiritual interpretation according to Mrs. Eddy.)

First it acknowledges God as supreme Father, and as our Father, everyone and every creature's Father. Our Father — caring for all. Then it hallows God's name, exalting it over all. "Thy kingdom come. Thy will be done in earth," here and now, for everyone and for every creature — the fullness of heaven, or harmony, expressed without limit, everywhere. "Give us this day our daily bread" is the full asking and receiving of the sum of grace and joy and goodness — and all needed supply. "And forgive us our debts, as we forgive our debtors." Mrs. Eddy's superb interpretation, "And Love is reflected in love," gives us God as divine Love controlling and expressing all human action. Love tenderly cherishing all that is living and expressing itself to man in all the universe — saving, protecting, blessing all creation. Surely that is heaven.

"And God leadeth us not into temptation, but delivereth us from sin, disease, and death." What can give or be more of heaven, more completely desirable, than that God is delivering all, everything, everywhere, from the evil one? "For Thine is the kingdom, and the power and the glory, . . . all Life, Truth, Love, over all, and All." And all this infinitely and forever. The heart of the Lord's Prayer is truly the entrance to heaven, and whoever acknowledges it, and honors and uses it, has the key to heaven.

This prayer has been most upon the lips of Christians because it is a prayer, a petition, declaration, assurance, full, complete and satisfying. This prayer has been the pathfinder for Christendom through the centuries. Perhaps its enduring vitality is because it makes no single claim for self. Even "Give us this day our daily bread; . . ." is not "Give me my bread," but "Give us our bread." It cares for all. It is for the universe and belongs to the universe. It saves the whole universe.

I have seen an instance of what the Lords' Prayer has done for just one man. You may enjoy hearing about it. Over thirty years ago he was an atheist, a radical, even taking the public platform against religion — an avowed infidel who believed religion to be a weakness. He was also a victim of alcoholism. One night he found himself in a Chicago hotel, in the extremity of *delirium tremens*. In his suffering, he discovered he was trying to recall the Lord's Prayer. He cursed himself for this, but soon he was trying to piece it together. Again he berated himself, but the prayer persisted. So on through the night until morning, in spite of himself, he had thought it all the way through. He also had resolved that if he lived until morning, he would seek out a Christian Science Reading Room, and try the help of Christian Science.

This he did.  From this help he became, in due time, a Christian Scientist.  And incidentally, in telling of this, he stated that it was the combined right thinking of all Christian Scientists which had so leavened human consciousness that the truth of Christ could reach him in that dark and desperate hour when he was truly tired of sin.  What encouragement for us, to keep on sending out right thinking!  And the angel of spiritual understanding reached this man in the form of the Lord's Prayer, which has for all these centuries moved as a stream of truth in human consciousness.  And which, in all his boastings against religion, this man had not been able to forget!

A number of years later, I saw this same man, by then a Christian Science practitioner, sit beside the bed of an aged woman who was very ill.  Delirium was beginning in a very trying form.  This Christian Scientist turned again to the Lord's Prayer, this time with the spiritual interpretation, as given in the Christian Science textbook, and going through it word by word, recalling its meaning and its healing power, he saw, by the time that prayer was finished, the healing of that belief of delirium.  Peace took its place; and again the power of the Word brought a touch of heaven.  And if this prayer twice did these blessed things for him, how much more his years of clinging to the Truth that it expresses has surely done much more for him in countless untold ways!

### Prayer in Action

Truth is ever-active in consciousness, and proceeds along the line of least resistance to belief.  Thus, man calls upon God for help, and at once establishes a connection between his thoughts and the utterance of Truth.

The action of this prayer, quickened by the understanding of Christian Science, illustrates what is working in human consciousness to bring heaven to mortals.  It shows that we think and act ourselves into heaven, by knowing and doing the will of God.

And this prayer is a great example of the correction of thought, which is the only thing that will ever get us into heaven. Correction of thought is the only way to heaven; and spiritually correct thoughts the only heaven. In our textbook we read, "Heaven is not a locality, but a divine state of Mind in which all the manifestations of Mind are harmonious and immortal, because sin is not there . . . ." Jesus' parable of the merchantman who, when he had found the pearl of great price, sold all that he had to buy it, typifies laying down all for heaven. Mrs. Eddy has wrought this into a rule of salvation, that is, "Self-renunciation of all that constitutes a so-called material man . . . is Science that opens the very flood-gates of heaven." (*Miscellaneous Writings*) One may have a farm, one may have a wife and so on, but it must all come secondary to one standard: *God first*. Correction of thought alone sells the lesser things, and buys heaven!

### Heaven Defined

In correcting thought, we learn what heaven is. We have been taught that the presence of God is heaven. God is everywhere; therefore heaven is everywhere. We do not die into heaven; we lift thought into heaven. In the 'Glossary' of our textbook we find this definition: "HEAVEN. Harmony; the reign of Spirit; government by divine Principle; spirituality; bliss; the atmosphere of Soul."

Let us consider these definitions for heaven further. One definition of "harmony" says, " . . . exquisite balance of the universe, the perfect relationship of part to part; the blend and interplay of joy, beauty, goodness, and happiness — all reflecting and reflecting themselves to constitute man's existence, and for man's forever enjoyment." Now the meaning of "the reign of Spirit" from our textbook definition, Spirit reigning over all means that all existence is ordered, governed by Spirit, God. Spirit reigning must determine the character of what it reigns over; must, by its reigning, establish its quality; must hold it by expressing always that which controls it. Therefore, there is no matter in Spirit's heaven.

Next we have "government by divine Principle" in our
continuing definition of "Heaven" — and isn't it marvelous to know
that man has a divine Principle by which to live? Just as a musical
chord has a basic principle, man has a source, origin, governor,
upon which he can call, with rules that are ordering or directing him
rightly — ruling out every discord of life with the exquisite harmony
of spiritual presence. The definition concludes with, "spirituality;
bliss: the atmosphere of Soul." Here we have a complete statement of the glory of perfection in all its forever infinite and beatific
loveliness! Christian Science reveals this as a present state of
man. That it is not to be died into, but it is to be wakened into. It
cannot be gone to someday, but must be lived up to, now, today.
The entire universe, including man, is a "receiving station" for God's
presence. When God looks into the mirror of divine Science, what
does He see? Himself, reflected, and that constitutes creation. To
rise mentally into this place of reflecting is our heaven — our dwelling
place in all generations. Unity with divine Mind is heaven. Stay
united to God and you cannot unite mentally with His opposite.

## Spiritual Man Understood and Lived

Do you regard yourself and others as material persons?
Do you think of yourself as a human person, going about material
things, and turning to Christian Science when you need help? Or
do you regard yourself always as a spiritual idea, incapable of being
mesmerized to see matter, sickness, death? Matter is not man,
never has been, never will be, and has nothing to do with man.
Neither has man anything to do with matter. Man is, our textbook
tells us, "the expression of God's being." "Man is idea, the image
of Love; he is not physique. He is the compound idea of God,
including all right ideas; . . ." The same page tells us what man is
not. "Man is not matter . . ." And we are taught plainly what he is
and what he is not. Then the one way to heaven is to correct
thought. The situation is wholly mental and all in our hands. We

are really, as Christian Scientists, about the business of lifting our own thoughts into heaven and so seeing all the universe as there. Your correcting of yourself helps by that much the whole world's correction. Watch your own thought. Where is it? What interests it? What fills it? What does it contemplate as real? And at every moment, when you find it doing anything else than exalting perfect God, perfect man, perfect universe — correct it. Bring it under the government of divine Principle. The din and discord of material sense cannot go with you into your highest point of prayer.

Christian Science already has corrected, basically, the thought of every one of us here. We have accepted the revelation which proclaims God as Spirit, and man and the universe as spiritual, which declares evil to have no place in God's creation, and which classifies all material sense as a counterfeit. The question is, "How far has this correction penetrated into the life, the affections, the personal behavior?" How much of this that we know is still only intellectual admission, and how much of it is actual regeneration? My own experience with the textbook statement, "If God is admitted to be the only Mind and Life, there ceases to be any opportunity for sin and death," is perhaps the experience of others. I read that for years. Yes, we admit it, grant it, accept it as being true. But that was simply an intellectual admission on my part.

The word *admit* burst upon me one day with meaning. Why "admit"? Admit means to let in; to receive; to take in. We wouldn't open our door to a person and say, "Yes, I admit you are here, and have the right to come in," and then shut the door upon him. We wouldn't call that exactly admitting him if we did it that way, even though we admitted that we saw him there. If we really admitted him, we would show him hospitality and welcome. We would make room for him, give him a place, and let him become a living part of the establishment. So, if God is admitted to be the only Mind and Life, there ceases, of course, "to be any opportunity for sin and death." If only intellectually admitted, with a "yes, I grant that this is so," sin and death can be hovering around here as much as ever. But if really admitted, let in, cherished, accepted in the affections, clung to and demonstrated, given the whole mental establishment to govern and correct, and that is the only full admission, then there really does cease to be any opportunity for sin and death! The admission that light is, doesn't put out the darkness; but admitting light itself, leaves no opportunity for darkness. In this correction of thought, a deeper pondering of that word *admit* may be of much help, as well as the phrase, "When God is admitted . . ."

## Correcting Thought

All education is correction of thought upon some point. All moral standards in our civilization, all standards in culture, art and education, in behavior and conduct, courtesy and consideration, are the things which enable human beings to stand one another. The spiritual perceptions upheld in the Scriptures, with the crowning stand of the Sermon on the Mount, have indeed brought the spiritual correction that embraces all lesser corrections. Mrs. Eddy's revealing God as divine Principle, and man the idea of that divine Principle, enables us to comprehend the scientific standard and rule for actually destroying sin, sickness, and death.

If man is mental, his Principle is the Principle of right thought, and works in understanding and correcting ignorance. Mrs. Eddy wrote of angels as "God's thoughts passing to man . . ." This statement points to the correction of thought in its uttermost regeneration. And each one of us knows in his own heart where and at what point this angelic correction should be going on.

Under the government of divine Principle, God and man are one. God and man act as one, or as someone else has put it, "The will of Mind is the action of the idea." Since we are that close to God, Mind wills the idea and man acts, performs, that will. In *No and Yes* we read, "God's laws, and their intelligent and harmonious action, constitute his [man's] individuality in the Science of Soul." Another way of saying, "The will of Mind is the action of the idea."

This unity of God and man constitutes heaven. And to point again to the correction of thought necessary to the Christian Scientist who would profit by this revelation, we quote again from the textbook, "The human thought must free itself from self-imposed materiality and bondage." "As a material, theoretical life-basis is found to be a misapprehension of existence, the spiritual and divine Principle of man dawns upon human thought . . ." We live in Mind; we do not live in body. We do not live in confusion, in restlessness. We live in heaven, as expressions of divine Mind.

## Christian Science Treatment Corrects Thought

Fundamentally, Christian Science treatment is prayer — prayer which begins with the recognition of a false claim, but which always ends with a realization of the ever-present heaven of celestial being, wherein is not a shadow of a false claim. Treatment rests in thought, in the pure sunlight of God's universe as it is, where not the slightest shadow can be known.

In the textbook Mrs. Eddy has written, "What renders both sin and sickness difficult of cure is, that the human mind is the sinner, disinclined to self-correction . . . " Let us look at correction of thought as it works through treatment — Christian Science treatment.

The right outlook upon existence is treatment, for treatment is the maintenance of a state of thought. It is spiritual understanding. And when that knowledge goes so far as to heal the sick, redeem the sinner, correct and spiritualize a life, then you have what the Christian Scientist calls a demonstration. A Christian Scientist is in himself, in his corrected life, only by as much as it is corrected, a constant state of treatment. When the Christian Scientist becomes that state of prayer and that state of behavior — that state of behavior, please mark, as well as that state of prayer — which exalts God and abolishes all evil, right there is a living example of Christian Science treatment!

Your bearing toward evil is your treatment of it. Your attitude toward preventing evil suggestions from entering your thinking, constitutes treatment. So belief in evil is treated by an ever increasing application of the understanding of the All-power of God, until the belief disappears. That the allness of God may be available to you, there are mental steps to be taken, something to be recognized and employed, a power to be utilized, a transaction to be undertaken and carried through, a process to be worked out, an application to be made, something to be done. And that something is to utilize the divine Mind through your reflection of it — to put to flight false beliefs.

And what about reflection? What about this boundless basis of Being, divine Mind? "God is at once," we are taught in *Science and Health*, "the centre and circumference of being." Divine Mind operates by the continuous impartation of itself to and through its ideas, ever conscious of itself and everything it knows. Impartation is not by subdivision or separation, but by reflection. Impartation means something going on. The reflected usage of this activity of divine Mind is the corrective thought which reaches to every part of the human experience. All experience is within the focal radius of the divine Mind, as the All-in-all bestows His own nature upon His own image and likeness.

In treatment whose thought do you correct? Your own, of course. Never anyone else's thought. That may follow, but your business is with your own thought. Your own corrected thought, looks out upon a perfect man, a perfect universe, God-governed, running in the grooves of a perfect heaven. Every prayer you pray, every treatment you give, or receive, every study hour, every conversation, should be correcting, lifting, cleansing, straightening your own thought, that you may maintain evenly and peacefully, with healing power, the right outlook upon creation.

What is the matter with us anyway, that after the vision of heaven opened to us by Christian Science, we should ever lag or sag or limp or whine? It is just that the human mind is disinclined to self-correction. We make our own way hard. We hold on to pet weaknesses, indulge appetites, cherish resentments and their unhappy brood. When "Out with them!" should be their quick destruction! If you see any Christian Scientist struggling, suffering, his thought way down in any way, you will find a lot of human viewpoints clogging his thinking, some sense of self hindering his thought. But lifted to the Truth of Being, the thinking will straighten out again.

Oh, if you can just come to love correction, be eager for it, seek for it in your sweet places of communion with God, you can by that communion be healed of this disinclination, and so greatly simplify the way to heaven.

Stop thinking like a faulty human and keep thinking as a divine idea. Remember, you are not the lump; you are the leaven; so keep thinking like the leaven. Whatever is in your thought, your home, business, friends, church, neighbor — think spiritually about them, be "leaven" to them.

Our Leader wrote in the textbook, "A mortal belief fulfils its own conditions." Then do not permit a mortal belief to fulfil its own conditions in your thought or experience. Divine Mind makes all the conditions for man. Beliefs do not govern, nor make conditions, nor fulfil their conditions for you, if you are constantly correcting them, putting them out of your own thought, and bringing your thinking under God's control.

I think, to advance in our healing work, we must come to see more clearly that matter is not substance. Come to realize that matter does not exist and cannot develop any alleged conditions. Mortals get afraid of their "alleged" bodies because they believe their bodies can do things to them apart from their thinking. But they cannot. "You embrace your body in your thought," according to the textbook.

Argument is very necessary. It is reasoning by which we convince ourselves of what is Truth and what is true; the reminder of the real and the rejection of the unreal. Argument is the ladder by which we climb.

Perhaps we are now spiritually minded enough to maintain some spiritual outlook without argument. I know that we are. But to protect the spiritual position and increase its strength, we surely need the continual reminder of the repeated Word of God. Our entire textbook is argument, in that it is a reasoning, an unfolding of the statement of Truth. The heavenly correction of thought through God's counter-acting "angels" must go on until there is nothing left to correct. You can't do without argument at every point. It is your strong tower!

Through the Scriptures and our Leader's writings, we must be divinely guided, each of us individually, to the right argument that will settle the thing in hand. That is why there can not be a formula for genuine Christian Science treatment. Spontaneity of thought should characterize every treatment. The great thing is to be a law that your treatment heals. Be the treatment. The great counter fact is the right idea of God, man, Life, health, and this has enough to heal. In *Science and Health* Mrs. Eddy writes, "The counter fact relative to any disease is required to cure it." The Bible and Mrs. Eddy's writings are gifts of God for instruction.

### *Spiritual Health*

The consistent follower of Christian Science is entitled to health, for health is a spiritual quality. As we put on spiritual under-standing, we correlatively put on health. Health itself is actually power to keep its opposite null and void. True health is spiritual; therefore it has power to enforce and maintain itself against the illusion of sickness. Health is God-like, and so is a permanent atti-tude of man. Thought that is "down" in matter takes on the load. Thought "up" in right ideas rolls off the load, freeing the body, for the body is just one's ability to "unsee" the general belief. And it can be done, for Godlike thinking wipes away false belief.

Surrender your personal sense to the government of Truth, and, although it is apparently and largely still personal sense, it becomes more harmonious even in its personal sense, because it is less error-governed, and more Truth-governed. The eraser of Christian Science treatment is busy rubbing out the mistaken mental position. That is the way Christian Science treatment works. You become less error-animated, more God-animated mentally, and everything adjusts to that.

## Acknowledging Improvement

In giving a treatment, a good thing to deal with directly is the reluctance of mortal mind to admit improvement. I think that is more fear than stubbornness. We must promise ourselves we will get well. A reluctance to promise would mean a reluctance to surrender to Truth; fear that healing won't come. It is always fear that prevents a promise, is it not? Full faith can always promise. In fact, the patient who can really promise to get well is holding no mental reservation, and right there he will find himself well. The reluctance to promise uncovers all the things which holds the patient's thought — fear, doubt and so on. How many of you right now can promise to get well at once, or come free at once of any trouble? That is a test question. Can you promise to give up that grudge, that fear, that self-pity, that personal domination? Can you promise to give up the pain? Don't try it on others; try it on yourself. Can you promise God to be well, happy, good and useful? If you can't, then find out what holds you from any such promises, and get rid of that. I once knew a deaf woman who would say instantly, "Yes, I know I am a spiritual idea and perfectly well in the Truth." But could you get her to acknowledge an improved belief, even when everyone else saw it? Well, only with difficulty. Are you ever that kind? The quick acknowledgment of improved belief means gratitude, obedience, spiritual perception, of finally letting go of fear.

## *Materiality an Illusion*

The great big thing asked of us as Christian Scientists, and the divinely simple thing, is that we shall always be realizing that materiality is illusion. We are asked to see it as illusion only, to keep it as illusion, to live above it as illusion. Any Christian Science treatment which does not have as its constant attitude the fact that all this fuss really isn't here at all, doesn't get very far. To the real man, it is never present. We love to turn to the statement in the textbook. "When the illusion of sickness or sin tempts you, cling steadfastly to God and His idea," because it starts us rightly at the outset; it places the trouble at once as illusion. Christian Science practice is really just a question of keeping the illusion as illusion, and upholding the spiritual fact as fact. We take this illusion of life in matter as something, reason and plan and act as if it were actually here, when the whole remedy lies in excluding it completely from thought through the power of reflection.

## *Handling Animal Magnetism*

The Christian Scientist's need is for handling the claim of animal magnetism. It is the specific name for all error, and Christian Science is here to dispose of it in consciousness. As we break the claim of animal magnetism, we soar and sing above our work. All Christian Science work is just undoing animal magnetism. Handling animal magnetism means going to heaven. It includes all the supposed conditions which perpetuate matter — the propagation, birth, maturity, decay of material organism, including man. It is the latent mental reservoir from which comes every woe. It is the one lying voice of animal magnetism which says:

*1. that it is mind or intelligence;*

*2. that it has stuff, substance, matter, out of which to make forms;*

13

*3. that it has space to put matter into — it has location;*

*4. that it has laws, causes, conditions, effects by which to destroy what it thinks it made;*

*5. that it has time in which to do destructive things;*

*6. that God created it and all its works — the most impudent claim of all.*

At this point in our own thinking, in our own temptation, we dissolve the dream with the Christ Truth. This dissolving goes on and the dream-world loses its hold just as fast as we see and prove error's illusive nature. Refusing to accept as real anything but perfect God, perfect man, and perfect universe, is the healing of animal magnetism; and when you have to go on taking care of things in the illusion — providing food and shelter and making concessions for it, and so on — you keep that watchword, illusion, in your thinking at every point. Keep the dream but without the dreamer. You know the stir against Christian Science is just part of the whole working out of salvation. Just world chemicalization. Christian Science "summons the conflict" with the dream stuff. Then we need not be dismayed by the dream chemicalization on all sides. It has been divinely summoned.

### Malpractice An Illusion

Then what of the alleged malpractice? First it would say it has to have a human thinker and a human object to think about, because mental malpractice can see only the output of its own belief. It creates for itself the instrument and object for its own victimizing. In Truth, the fact of creation is reflection. The lie about creation is objectification. The lie must have an object in belief because it lacks reflection. There is no material man. The alleged mental malpractitioner simply directs his efforts at his own belief that man is material. So live then, as a spiritual idea, where you can neither be hit by any stones, or throw them.

The entire fabrication called *malpractice* is an illusion, null and void! Mrs. Eddy states in *Science and Health*, "Mortals are inclined to fear and to obey what they consider a material body more than they do a spiritual God." Suddenly my thought was arrested in this textbook statement, by the word *consider*. Mortals fear and obey what they consider a material body. Man, body, identity, are all spiritual. Mortal belief simply objectifies itself and considers that mental objectification to be a material body. This leaves no sinner and no victim.

It has been well said that Christian Science fits us to live in the storm. It does this by showing us that the storm is illusion. The moment we let error become real to us, we have let in the storm. We keep it without, and so live in spite of it. We need to know what is darkening the mental sky, locally and universally. It is not to be ignored, but always overcome in obedience to the rule that your mind shall not be filled with it, but filled with Truth and Love. You do not study the unreality. You study the Truth. Truth uncovers error. Truth does it. So cling to Truth, and let it summon the conflict, and wait on God. When you see error of any kind, you summon your battalions of angels and displace it promptly. The memory of wrongs, evils, failures, must yield its ghost to these angels of Truth which show that error never really happened, nor made history.

Let me give an illustration of Mrs. Eddy's handling of a situation. A student was talking with Mrs. Eddy, telling our Leader how her husband was suffering from injuries received in the Civil War. Mrs. Eddy quickly asked, "What war?" The lady explained, "Why the Civil War." Mrs. Eddy again asked, "What war?" Again the explanation, "Why the Civil War between the North and South."

Still the same question, "What war?" but she added, "I see you both believe there was a war." With that, the light broke through. Christian Science treatment itself stands firmly on the ground that to God and the real man, evil never occurs! Remember Christian Science is the leaven because it knows the unreality of all error, and that the leaven is working in the lump. What persons present of error, you must unsee as a system. You deal with the whole of evil, not just its representative.

## Living Love

Our burning zeal should be to see our brother saved from error, never condemned in it. As time goes on and we see Christian Scientists' efforts and needs, we are sometimes forced to the conclusion that we are very long in being scientific and very short on loving consideration, courteousness — the little things which go to make one another healthier and happier. In our very desire to do the right, we are sometimes afraid to be decently courteous, human, and tender. We have all come to realize that man is dear to God. But do we as quickly make as our own, the companion truth that man is dear to man? A quotation from an article by Elizabeth Harrison, is appropriate here, "The men who are lifting the world upward are those who encourage more than criticize." Matthew Arnold says, "Culture is the ability to recognize the best in others."

Man is always all right. All we need to do is to correct our own thought about man. We need time and quiet to ponder the things of God. Birds can sing on the wing, but they also rest on the branches and sing. And they tuck themselves in, out of the storm. So you should have frequent times for being tucked in, out of the storm; times for study, for quiet prayer. I once heard a lovely story I'd like to share. An orthodox minister, one whose field of endeavor was with the so-called down-and-outs of the world, that is, the unemployed, discouraged, and sinful, told this story to a group of people: "You know, when a man starts off to his work in the morning, he takes long strides, vigorous and strong, covering the ground quickly. However, when he returns home at night, if his little girl comes down the street to meet him, he takes her hand in his, and then shortens his step, makes it just as short and slow as the little girl needs it to be, to walk with him. And you know, that is the way God walks with us, and lets us walk with Him. He takes the shorter steps we need to have, that He might keep right beside us and we may keep up with Him. Nothing is too small or too slow for God to walk with, if it is really striving to walk with Him." One of our Christian Science hymns says this beautifully, "The God who made both heaven and earth, And all that they contain, Will never quit His steadfast truth, Nor make His promise vain." He takes the short steps.

Our great need is to increase our faith — increase our trust. This is brought out in a story from *The American* magazine: A father took his two children out to swim, a girl of ten and a boy younger. Way out in the water he recognized that, while they were all good swimmers, the children were too tired to swim back, and the difficulties were too great for him to take them both in at the same time. So he said to his ten-year old girl something like this, "I am going to take your brother in, and then I will come back for you. You know how to float, so just do that. Do not try to swim or get anywhere, just float and rest until I come back." And with that he bravely left her out in the water. He just barely got in with the boy, and told his story. Dozens sprang to his help, and several boats put out. They found the little speck of humanity out on the water, having floated along for three hours. When they lifted her tenderly into the boat, she was very tired, but not at all frightened, for she said, "Daddy said he would come back for me and Daddy keeps his word." God always keeps His Word.

Serenity should always characterize the Christian Scientist. To give rest to the body, the mentality must be right, must be casting out all that contributes to unrest. It is peace, serenity and trust that can be giving rest to the body. Your own purified mentality gives you rest. It is divine Mind which makes us, sustains us, for it is ever renewing us, ever replenishing us as the sun renews its light and warmth.

There is no death for man. This constant divine renewal keeps man ever living — he cannot die. And the shadow that says he dies, is just an illusion. Even if we seem to see our dear ones touched by this shadow, we know they are not sinking into it, but walking across it. You cannot bury thought. You never have buried one you love, for that one was, and is, a thinker. God must be admitted to be the whole of life in order to correct thought. Remember, all problems are solved by an absolute stand in Truth; and in their solving, the human adjustments settle themselves rightly under the power of reflection. Disinclination to correct thought must be watched and dealt with.

I close with a passage from *Science and Health*: "The elements and functions of the physical body and of the physical world will change as mortal mind changes its beliefs. What is now considered the best condition for organic and functional health in the human body may no longer be found indispensable to health. Moral conditions will be found always harmonious and health-giving. Neither organic inaction nor over-action is beyond God's control; and man will be found normal and natural to changed mortal thought, and therefore more harmonious in his manifestations than he was in the prior states which human belief created and sanctioned

"As human thought changes from one stage to another of conscious pain and painlessness, sorrow and joy, — from fear to hope and from faith to understanding, — the visible manifestation will at last be man governed by Soul, not material sense."

# THE POWER OF AN ENDLESS LIFE
## Association Address of 1928

We are going to open our thought today, I trust, to a larger inpouring of what Paul's letter to the Hebrews calls "the power of an endless life."

Everyone knows that he is living, that he is alive. Only the Christian Scientist knows, is aware, that he is now living a life unseen to the material senses, a life that expresses spiritual power, and which is endless. Without the light of Christian Science, mortals believe they live as perishable matter bodies and then later — after an incident called 'death' — that they are transformed into spiritual being. With the light of Christian Science, we know that we are spiritual beings now; that we always have been, are now, and always will be spiritual beings and nothing else. As God's image, the real and only man is as immortal now as he ever will be; whatever is going to be immortal is immortal now, and is here, and is your real selfhood.

So we are here today for further spiritual education concerning immortality, for a renewal, a revival, in the power of an endless life. The particular words spoken shall be words of Truth that cut through the mesmeric dullness, and reassure thought as to spiritual facts. We cannot hear the words of Truth too often. They do not necessarily repeat, but constantly restate. What is the constant treatment in which we stand but the continuous re-statement of Truth clung to and trusted? And what does this Word do except to de-mesmerize thought and bring to light man's present immortality. The whole purpose of an association meeting is to de-mesmerize thought, to arouse and clarify spiritual insight. Every treatment you give is to de-mesmerize thought, your own thought. And this is done by the re-statement of the living Word of God. Truth will re-state itself to all eternity. The continuing re-statement of Truth goes on in spiritualizing consciousness and constitutes the constant awareness of Truth which is itself true consciousness. Our day together here should de-mesmerize and free thought from its belief in perishable mortality and plant us more firmly in our immortality, our demonstration of the power of an endless life.

### *Mortal Life Unreal*

All the life you think you have lived in matter has not been life at all; only a dream blur. Discordant, sordid, selfish, fearful, afflicted, it is only a dream blur. All this time when belief has believed that dream, you have been living an immortal life, have been experiencing in God's sight an endless life in Him. Learn to identify the 'you' that you think of as yourself with the spiritual idea which God knows. Don't regard yourself as a mortal calling upon Truth for help, but know yourself now as an immortal, the living exponent of Truth — of the power of an endless life. Your Life is in Christ, in the demonstration of God, never at all in the falsities called matter; and there in Christ you can be aware of your endless life if you let the constant re-statement of Truth rule your thought and rule out of it all that would mesmerize and darken.

In our present sense of existence we do not escape problems. Christian Scientists live in the same world with all other humans. They have the same problems. No one escapes them. But the Christian Scientist has this great advantage — he knows the rule and has the light by which to solve the problems. We don't escape them; we solve them with God's help. So, we stop asking "Why does this come to me?" and we go to work.

Going to work, our chief interest centers in the power of that rule and that light to dispel evil and enlarge good. When we apply that rule and walk in that light, we call our conscious effort in that direction Christian Science treatment.

## The Power of Treatment

Our mental effort is to let the Truth re-state itself to us, and that re-statement, clung to, obeyed, accepted in life-practice, constitutes treatment. Christian Science treatment is the sincere, intelligent acknowledgment of the power and presence of God to offset the lying voices of personal sense. But the question is — do we know and trust the power invoked by true Christian Science treatment? We all know how to give the treatment; we have the letter; we strive to live the life of a Christian. But it is my growing conviction that many Christian Scientists don't begin to know the actual power of what they cherish and declare. One of our big pitfalls, I think, is our own belief that we can give treatment over and over with delayed or very little result. Our own lack of trust in the power of treatment — this is our stumbling block. What is the trouble? Lack of faith.

We don't cultivate faith so much as we de-mesmerize our thought from fear through uniting our thought with God. Then we find the faith spontaneously springing up in us, for we reflect in divine Mind our faith and our confidence in good, just as we reflect everything else that we are. Faith in God's power must come as we think as God thinks, for in so thinking, thought is one with power. Christian Science lived, individualizes infinite power, and that constitutes being a Christian Scientist.

The how — how to express this power, how to experience it, how to become established in it, how to find ourselves deeply trusting it, surely expecting it, always confident that it is here, knowing that it works, and works to deliver and heal and comfort and save to the uttermost — that is our deep-down desire, and that is our task. Our Master and our Leader have given us two exact, unfailing rules that will, as they are worked out, establish divine power as

Emmanuel — God with us.  These rules are — "Be ye therefore perfect, even as your Father in heaven is perfect," and "The good you do and embody gives you the only power obtainable."  Not the letter you have, not the good you theorize about — but the good you do and embody.  The good you let in — and actually embody — is what you are.

## The Power of Spiritual Goodness

We all manifest some spiritual good; more perhaps than we know.  Some unselfishness, some purity, justice, honesty, kindness.  And if we can only know that that good is power because it is God reflecting Himself, we have laid hold of heavenly help.  "Honesty is spiritual power," our textbook says.  So, by divine logic, purity and selflessness and loving-kindness are themselves power, because they are divine attributes and so individualize infinite power.  We should really have the sense to know that fact at all times, but Beelzebub claims to rob us of our sense of this sometimes, and we fall into believing that we can express all the good we know how, and yet suffer and fail.  But good is power — power to rout suffering and failure — because it is God expressed.  Spiritual goodness is power, and so as goodness is expressed, power is expressed.  God is power and all power, so God reflected is power reflected.  Truth and power are one.  Love and power are one.  The warmth of Love is power to adjust all things.  Good and power are one.  Our whole lifework is to express God in exquisite heavenly goodness, and then trust the power shining through that goodness to establish the will of God, the will of good.  Expressed goodness will heal and save as God intends it shall do.

Our whole education is to divest thought of any belief that evil is power, and to de-mesmerize thought that it shall not fear evil.  Keep your thought constantly reminded and reassured that evil is not power, and that God, good, is all power.  Then express all the God you can in a loving, right life, and you are expressing all of the power you can. If Love is reflected in love, if Life is reflected in life, if God is reflected in goodness, then the divine might which upholds the universe is reflected in the power of the Word, according to your goodness, and your treatment will be power and will prevail. The dynamic power of the Word is always with the Word when it is spoken through a Christian life.

God, expressing Himself as Christ, His Son, His manifestation, His reflection, is All-power, for God and His reflection constitute what is — eternal, indestructible, true being. God maintaining His universe, reflecting Himself to Himself as man and the universe, upholding and blessing all His infinity of creation, is the power of an endless life.

The divine continuance, perpetuity, foreverness of the universe, shows forth the power of divine Mind. To keep a reflection, a creation, endlessly going and never stopping, is certainly power. Eternal foreverness is something that can never lapse nor break down, and so the continuing endlessness of true being expresses the power of it. Power to sustain creation forever is divine might itself, divine being itself, and that mighty thing is the endless power upon which all true being rests and upon which all true prayer calls.

### One Governing Power

Power means also government. That which is power governs. To avoid chaos there must be one governing power. And so if the good we live individualizes infinite power, the good we live also governs, for power governs. The good you do and embody, governs all that concerns you, for it expresses God — the one Governor. If we want God's protection we must express the qualities which God protects. The good you do and embody brings protection with it.

What keeps the sun shining; the stars wheeling; the seasons returning; the verdure growing; the vapors gathering and descending? Surely neither you nor I nor any man has the slightest thing to do with that. And that same power and government which maintains a universe keeps your eyes seeing, your ears hearing, your functions acting, your business and home blossoming, your happiness constant, your whole being harmonious. From the same source whence comes the balancing of the clouds, and the constancy and beauty of the sunrise, comes your strength, health, happiness and completeness. All you have to do is to link your thought and living with it. Christian Science has rent the veil which hides this splendid fact and awakens us to see, understand and yield to this divine power and divine government, and so possess here and now more and more of this power of an endless life. Human consciousness kept in constant relation with the divine individualizes infinite power.

*Scientific Treatment Illustrated*

All this reliance upon the power of God constitutes, of course, Christian Science treatment. We have just been giving thought to the Christian aspect of treatment — the embodiment of good which insures power. So now let us look at what we might call the scientific aspect of treatment. As we have said here before, there are several fundamental things to know about Christian Science treatment, and knowing them, spiritual intuition will then guide our thought in every instance to a complete and effectual treatment.

First, that treatment has foundation, origin, source, and basis in the allness of God, for it is the living Word of God. Next, that treatment has forward-going action in the spiritual activity of the right idea, which through prayer is individualizing the power of the Word. Next, that treatment has direction because its reflected power wipes out the particular falsity which has called forth the treatment. And next, that treatment has protection in the vitality of its own Word as power or infinite enforcement of itself to prevail over all hindrances.

We can approach this in another way, and say that treatment includes knowing the Truth about the three specific things. The truth about God, the truth about man, and the truth about error. The truth about God is His infinite Allness. The truth about man is his forever spiritual perfection. The truth about error is its nothingness — its past, present and future nothingness. There is nothing really interesting to us about error except its nothingness.

Suppose we sketch right here a treatment based upon those three fundamental facts. First we have the truth about God, stated for us in our textbook, as incorporeal, divine, supreme, infinite Mind. Incorporeal, or bodiless, divine in nature, supreme in that He rules all, infinite in never-ending and all-encompassing existence — and all this as Mind. Mind is consciousness — that which is capable of saying to itself, "I AM." God is the divine, supreme, infinite, everywhere present "I AM."

Next, according to our textbook, God is Spirit; the divine substance which is the exact opposite of matter. Next, Soul, the divine perceptive and comprehensive faculties which are the direct opposite of personal sense. Next, divine Principle, the source and origin, the unfailing, unerring, all encompassing, all-enveloping maintainer and container of all existence. "The centre and circumference of being," *Science and Health* tells us. Next, Life, which is the animation, the active, never-stopping conscious identity. Next, Truth, the rock of unchanging dependability. Next, Love, that which tenderly wills all happiness and bliss to everything which lives. Just think of this, that the will of Love to preserve and bring joy to everything is enforced by Principle, Soul, Spirit, Life and Truth, is enforced by unfailing power.

All this divinity, infinity, omnipotence, wills that all creation shall be right and happy. It is animated by the tenderness which always bestows all bliss, and must bestow it by reason of its power. The definition of God in the 'Glossary' of *Science and Health*, defines Him as: "The great I AM: the all-knowing, all-acting, all-seeing, all-wise, all-loving and eternal. . . ."

His all-knowing knows only good and is everywhere, and so excludes any knowing of evil. His all-seeing and all-hearing exclude any seeing or hearing of evil so far as true Mind is concerned. His all-acting makes it impossible for falsity to act anywhere in His universe. And His eternal all-wise and all-loving nature preserves creation intact and happy. This is a hint of the Truth about God, and to turn to it for refuge brings reassurance and healing always. Truth, re-stated, heals.

In *Miscellaneous Writings*, Mrs. Eddy refers to her discovery as, "The prism of divine Science." Just as the prism used in experiments with light reveal the white ray of light to be composed of the seven primary colors, so the prism of divine Science, Christian Science, through which we all look at God, reveals the completeness of God through the different synonyms for God which Mrs. Eddy uses. So we may, stating her seven synonyms, conclude that God, being Mind, takes care of His creation with infinite intelligence. God being Spirit, takes care of His creation spiritually, without material accompaniments. God as Soul endows His creation with perceptive faculties for the enjoyment of beauty and of all that is lovely. God as Principle, holds creation within His own Allness and governs all He contains. God as Life perpetuates His creation in endless being. God as Truth is infinite dependability and cares for all He knows with sublime integrity, and God as Love tenderly gathers in all that lives, loving its welfare, wanting infinitely to promote for it all bliss and blessedness. God cares for His creation because He has to and because He wants to, being Mind, Spirit, Soul, Principle, Life, Truth and Love. Mrs. Eddy continues her statement about "the prism of divine Science" which reveals these hues of Deity by adding: "The lens of Science magnifies the divine power to human sight; and we then see the supremacy of Spirit and the nothingness of matter."

We next have the truth about man. He is reflection, expression, manifestation, emanating from God. Emanation means a flowing forth; an issuing forth as from a source, as sunlight from the sun. And because of the nature of his inexhaustible source, man is a continuing emanation, ever-appearing. Man at the meridian of perfect being, knowing neither birth nor death, is constantly renewed from his infinite source. Man exists at the meridian of perfect being and is constantly replenished from his divine origin and center, always flowing forth, or shining forth, in the activity of reflection, a perpetual witness to the infinity of the Mind within which, as idea, he forever lives. That man can have no trouble. He cannot lack any good thing. He cannot be deceived or robbed or harmed; he knows no mortality; he lives in the exquisite joy of an indestructible, harmonious life of Spirit. And to the degree right now that you "put on" that man, you have all the joy that goes with him, for he is not made after the law of a carnal commandment, but after the "power of an endless life." To quote further from Hebrews: "Without father, without mother, without descent, having neither beginning of years nor end of days, but made like unto the Son of God." This is something of the truth about man.

The whole mistake about existence is what Mrs. Eddy calls "a finite sense of the infinite." Finiteness is the error. Infinity is the truth. Being is all here, immortal, indestructible. Being is infinite. But a finite sense of the infinite would, of course, make infinite being appear finite, having beginning and end, and including all the horrors and desolation that would go on with limiting and ending.

I think a perfectly complete treatment would be given in the realization that there is no finite sense of the infinite. That would free thought from mortal limitation and reveal the infinite facts. A finite sense of the infinite is the error to be outgrown. The finite sense is about something, and that something is the infinite being that is right here, real man and the universe. Creation is and is all here! Being is limitless, boundless, infinite. And Christian Science is abolishing the finite sense of creation, the mist that went up from the earth, and is revealing the infinite reality.

Last we have the truth about error and its nothingness. Our Leader once wrote, "A million naughts never made a number." Error is always negation — nothingness. It never really happened. You cannot experience error, for it is never experience. It never gets to be a positive quantity, and so it can't be experienced. At most it is only a dream blur, always a negation. It may parade and mutter and threaten, but it does not perform. It may talk, but it never acts. It may boast, but it never gets beyond the boast. It cannot become manifestation or phenomenon, because it has no entity, no substance, no being, in the sight of God, and it should have less and less in our sight. At most, error is nothing more than suggestion, whisper, mirage, illusion, supposition, false belief, lie. Error is lifeless, truthless, powerless, substanceless nothing. Mrs. Eddy writes in the textbook, " . . . the human mind never produced a real tone nor sent forth a positive sound." And that's the truth about error.

So the truth about those things — God, man, and error — constitute a good treatment, one that will work to the extent that it is the spirit with us and not just the letter.

## The Healing Effects of Treatment

You have the right to less and less error and more and more good in your experience all the time. The right to become established in good. As you separate error from your thought of man, you are entitled to a higher, purer sense of living in all directions — more abundance of God, less aggression of evil. Your exclusion of error from your thinking entitles you to exclusion of error from your sight, your hearing, your experience. So error is "handled," as we say in Christian Science. It is not ignored or whitewashed. Like a serpent, it is brought out of its hole, recognized by its name, dealt with concretely by thorough treatment, and when reduced to nothing, becomes nothing to you, and then cannot appear to you.

Mrs. Eddy also writes in the textbook, "Because God is Spirit, evil becomes more apparent and obnoxious proportionately as we advance spiritually, until it disappears from our lives." First, the cleavage between good and evil; the keener spiritual insight detecting it more swiftly and surely; and then, its complete disappearance from thought and experience.

The entire success of your treatment is established as you make evil null and void. The truth about error is its nullness and voidness, and that is the only truth there is about it. All the hydra-headed claims of evil are in God's sight null and void. So as they become null and void to you, you have won out. There is no animal magnetism; it has no hatred to obstruct Truth, no conditions, instruments, persons, places or objects, single or collective, educated or malicious, to assail the well-being of man, for it is all null and void. It has no principle, basis, presence, action, for it is null and void. That which is null and void has no location. Null means without character, significance, force or validity; void means empty, vacant, destitute — a vacuum. So your constant song should be null and void — null and void — as the truth about error. And the truth of error as null and void delivers you from believing it. Even though it passes before you as a moving picture, it is null and void — and your fidelity in sticking right there delivers you.

## De-personalizing Animal Magnetism

In this Christian and scientific process of proving the nothingness of nothing, animal magnetism is well defined when we see that its entire nature is expressed in mental suggestion and through the instrument of personal contagion. All three phases of animal magnetism — the ignorant, the educated, and the malicious — must have channels or persons through which to suggest itself. All educated erroneous systems of belief must be sponsored and propagated by persons. All influences for evil act hypnotically through personal contact or contagion. So deprive animal magnetism of its personal exponents or channels, de-personalize animal magnetism, and you disarm it utterly. It cannot use God's ideas; and when you see the unreality of personalities, you leave it nothing to use. Animal magnetism could not claim to exist had it not persons supposedly to think, talk and act through. Mesmeric mental suggestion from person to person and group to group by means of mass education and mental mob influence, is the method of animal magnetism. It could not operate without persons as instruments. The impersonal evil, or devil, uses the thoughts, tongues, hands and feet of persons. As divine Mind expresses itself through its individual ideas, so animal magnetism claims to express itself through its counterfeit of divine ideas — namely, human personality.

Years ago Mrs. Eddy wrote to someone, "It is as necessary to know there is no personality as to know there is no sin." In the realm of Spirit there are no channels, mediums or persons. Those are all human concepts. We say we are channels for good. A Christian Science hymn says, "Make channels for the streams of Love." Well and good, if we remember that channels and mediums and windowpanes are all on the dream side of the question. They are thinner spots in the dream. But even they disappear with the rest of the dream, for in the divine universe reflection is complete everywhere. "Mind is its own interpreter," through reflection of Himself to and through every idea, completely. So there are no mediators in heaven. As you cease then, to think of yourself or anyone else as a channel or mediator, you liberate yourself and others from the whole fabric of personal contagion. Exalting thought above the personal sense of existence, you exalt it above animal magnetism — or personal contagion.

Mrs. Eddy certainly knew about this, and an examination of what she has written about personal contagion gives us much light. She exposes it in many instances, for the dependence upon person hides and prevents dependence upon Principle. In *Miscellany*, under the caption "Personal Contagion," she writes, "This great truth of God's impersonality and individuality and of man in His image and likeness, individual, but not personal, is the foundation of Christian Science." There never was a religion or philosophy lost to the centuries except by sinking its divine Principle in personality. May all Christian Scientists ponder this fact and give their talents and loving hearts free scope only in the right direction. She appeals to Christian Scientists to leave her free for the divine ascent. Again she states in *Miscellany*, "Thinking of persons implies that one is not thinking of Principle." And in the same book, "Had the ages helped their leaders to, and let them alone in God's glory, the world would not have lost the Science of Christianity."

You may be sure that as you wipe out your own sense of being a mediator or channel, or a personal practitioner, to make it specific, you take down your target. Believing that you are somebody or something sets up a target for reaction. It is as important to know there is no personal practitioner as to know there is no personal patient. It dissolves together, leaving no patient, no channel, no target, but just the forever fact of God's perfect ideas. Every one of us has to get rid of an egotistical personal selfhood which would like to be a channel, but which is itself the only target there is for malpractice. As you take down your sense of yourself as somebody, you give up your sense that you are somebody to be malpracticed upon. In de-personalizing animal magnetism, depersonalize yourself first of all. Unsee a mortality and physicality calling itself by your name. Live as a spiritual idea, and never think of yourself in any other terms than spiritually. I often wonder why any of us ever think of ourselves or anyone else or anything else except in the terms of the power of an endless life, when we know that through such thinking the door of deliverance opens to us.

We are malpracticing upon ourselves, holding ourselves down, when we regard ourselves as human — holding an image in thought that is subject to temptation, lack, sorrow, sin, disease, death, a veritable target for all error. Thinking in divine terms of ourselves and others, keeping aware of all God's creation as it is, stops our malpractice upon ourselves and others, and takes away any supposed target that the thoughts of others can supposedly malpractice upon.

I know of a prominent Christian Scientist, engaged in very important work, who was overwhelmed by responsibility and fear of failure, until another Scientist whom he highly respected said to him, when he was told of the trouble, "Oh, you aren't so much." Instantly the personal selfhood collapsed, and he had no more trouble. He was healed from the inside — not by any change on the outside. I know another man doing conspicuous work in the movement who said, "Why, error isn't doing anything to me just because I'm doing this work. All I can put down to malpractice is that I lost a handkerchief a few days ago, and I know where that is and expect to get it back again," That is a healthy state of thought for a Christian Scientist. And that was due to true humility. That man couldn't feel so free unless he were wrapping himself about in the garments of humility. He had taken down his target. So, through unselfing our thinking, we take down ours.

Our Leader exposes another phase of personal contagion when she writes in the *Church Manual*, "Neither animosity or mere personal attachment should impel the motives or acts of the members of The Mother Church." Mere personal attachment! The mere personal attachment which blinds us to the faults of friends like the animosity which balloons the faults of the unfriendly and disliked, is all the same error — all personal. And it must yield to divine Principle. To think and act clearly from the basis of Principle is what the Christian Scientist has set out to do. At our heels is a clever robber. It steals away our study hours, our seasons of prayer, our opportunities for spiritual pondering, and for divine listening. Catching at our weak points and mesmerizing us along the lines of least resistance, it gets us sometimes engulfed in over-personal associations with friends, tangled in personal contagion.

### Friendship and Solitude

The times are strenuous for most of us. Daily life is busy. It takes watching and acting to get a minimum of time apart from the routine and the crowd. A large balance of prayer is needed. We have all learned to pray and run, but there must be times when the running lets up and all the attention goes to praying. Now, we must not misunderstand this. Some friendship is precious and price-less. Our Leader writes in *Retrospection and Introspection*, "There are no greater miracles known to earth than perfection and an unbroken friendship." And in *Miscellany* she writes, "It is only by looking heavenward that mutual friendships such as ours can begin and never end." God is the great Friend to all creation, and we must reflect His tender friendliness to each other. Life must be lived through the eyes of the heart to find brotherhood and heaven. Human duties must be lovingly done; human kindnesses shown; human responsibilities never left to burden others. Our lives should be full of the little human kindnesses, for that is divine Love in action, divine Love going forward. But that is a totally different thing from the mesmerism of dependence upon the human pres-ence of others. There is no weaker person than he who cannot bear to be alone. There is no stronger person than the one who finds his power in solitude.

In her *Message to The Mother Church of 1901*, Mrs. Eddy writes, "The Christian Scientist is alone with his own being and the reality of things." Mortal mind says that you must have matter about in order to be conscious of presence or companion-ship. Christian Science says you must be alone with God and His idea in order to have the companionship of infinity — the infinity of man and the universe. You can have a lonesome belief among a thousand people, or you can have a contented understanding with God, quite apart from people. To be with what senses tell us of companionship is to have nothing enduring. In fact, the social pres-ence is often no more than a social stimulant which is followed by the reaction and let-down which follows all stimulants.

The pressure of faces and voices often prevents the quiet contemplation of the infinite. It keeps before us an acute sense that existence is personal, whereas our whole calling now as Christian Scientists is to impersonalize our sense of existence. We must and do love our friends, value and serve them. But that is very different from having to constantly be with them. We all know the joy of loving and cherishing our friends when we are quiet and alone and can think about them in the way that holds them and ourselves up to God, in the realities of an endless life. Not in material contact, but in spiritual understanding we have our friends, as we have all things.

In his essay on "Friendship," Ralph Waldo Emerson says some fine and true things: "It is foolish to be afraid of making one's ties too spiritual," he writes, "as if we could lose any genuine love. . . . Let us even bid our friends farewell, and defy them, saying, 'Who are you? Unhand me, I will be dependent no more.' Ah, seest thou not, oh brother, that thus we part only to meet in a higher platform and only be more each other's because we are more our own?"

The great thinkers have always struggled against personal contagion, which is the direct opposite of the brotherhood of man, and Mrs. Eddy has certainly called us up and out of it. In the solitary prayer and fasting which annuls our own animosity, we find that which gives light and healing to our friends and to the world. In aimless, pointless human associations, pleasant though they may be, and enjoy them as we may, we find that which keeps existence personal to us, and darkens healing.

Surely you will not mistake any of this as decrying true friendship. It exalts it. To weave the thread of life with a friend, in word or in deed, is one thing; to indulge the mesmerism of the social stimulant is quite another thing. Tolerance, forbearance, goodwill, tender consideration, ministering affection, all spring from those spiritual ties which truly bind friend to friend, while selfish demands, disappointments, hurts, characterize personal contagion. True affection is life. Loving is living. The joy of right loving constitutes being; but human emotions, and the clutch and grab of personal contagion, are the exact opposite of love.

Nor does this mean that normal human recreation should not be ours. Whatever keeps your thought rested and close to God is right for you, and Christian Scientists differ greatly in their capacity to be with people and still keep their poise. We can't judge for each other, but must watch for ourselves. We cannot withdraw from the stream of human living — for it is right here together that we solve the human problem. To do the loving service with hands and feet is to make love practical. We don't run away, but we demand from our friends opportunity for that solitude of thought wherein true being is pondered, and from which we can return to them more helpfully. We can, if we honestly want it, come to discriminate between the healing human kindnesses which are life itself, and the personal contagion which would smother life, for the personal sense of existence must go out before the impersonal.

We can be good believers in Christian Science, and yet remain very materially minded. We can drift and dream, instead of reflect. But that won't do. We must spiritualize actual thought-habits and watch what we think about and how we think about it. Quiet seasons of solitude and prayer stabilize and clarify and strengthen us as nothing else can do. This all really should work out for us according to divine law. If you know everyday that divine Mind knows where you are, and can find you and use you, and that mortal mind cannot discover or locate or use you, all your contacts and associations will surely be helpful and right. That to which you can be useful under God's ordering, would find you; things which would waste and scatter you, can't find you. Some kind of mind must operate to bring about every contact you have, and as you prove that only the Christ-Mind has presence or power to act, you will, of course, elevate your entire experience, associations, and contacts. Right desire and right mental work certainly should be bringing this about.

I have had a good deal to say about this, for I think we need it. In *Retrospection and Introspection* we find this statement by our Leader: "Mind demonstrates omnipresence and

35

omnipotence, but Mind revolves on a spiritual axis, and its power is displayed and its presence felt in eternal stillness and immovable Love. The divine potency of this spiritual mode of Mind, and the hindrance opposed to it by material motion, is proven beyond a doubt in the practice of Mind-healing. We can learn to lay down the hindrance of material motion for the eternal stillness and immovable Love."

## Conclusion

Now, we apparent humans who are calling ourselves Christian Scientists, are just like all humans. Our great advantage over the others is that we see the way out of mortality. We have started on that way. We are where the Truth corrects and adjusts false beliefs, because we are seeing the Truth and letting it in. So we get, in belief, improved beliefs of life, or beliefs thinned more and more of materiality. Truth is brought to bear upon error, and so a Christian Scientist earns adequate protection. He knows that in Truth he is all right. But he also knows that if he clings to Truth, he need not be even humanly over-taxed, over-strained, over-burdened, for if his motive is right, Christian Science applied, sustains even his present belief in increasing freedom from error. That is how Christian Science heals; and if it didn't sustain and improve your present belief, right now and here, it wouldn't be worth any more than a theory. Christian Science works through honest motive — that is the open door — to give you a happier, healthier, better supplied human sense until the human disappears. And this we can see is logical, because the knowledge of Truth abolishes the fear and liking for evil, a fear and a liking which have nipped and cramped and warped the body and the affairs of humans. Error dropped from thought lets go of the body and the affairs of humans. Error is thus proven null and void, so we have improved beliefs right now, even though we have only started on our journey.

This being true, we can expect to become more and more

established in our demonstration of good — to have reassurance, settled convictions, certain answers to prayer, fruition. I was much interested to hear an able Scientist say recently that she thought the next generation would have a very different sense of Christian Science practice because of their constant reading of *Science and Health*. The conclusion from this is that thought will broaden to a larger sphere, and to a wider outlook at the human problem — will come to see humanity as one, and work along more general and less personal lines. Be less busy with a personal sense of problems and patients, and more free to work and pray in larger strokes for the entire race. The things which concern universal brotherhood will be increasingly expanding our thought up and out of the personal. The habits of fear and self-interest will yield to concern for the welfare of all, and trust in good will become more natural and habitual. Even now we can, to the degree we know our own sincerity, wrap ourselves about with God's mercies and feel established in them. Christian Science offers all that human want and suffering and longing can possibly think of, wish for, or need — bliss, health, happiness, dominion, infinity of good.

And the fruit of honest labor will largely be established with us now. You become established in music, mathematics, all the arts and sciences — anything to which you give honest devotion; then why not become established in good, with its sweet securities? Healing, supply, spiritual success, should be established with you now. As you put down fear and sin, you have every right to expect them to be yours. You can trust God to be Himself and to be everywhere.

This is generally made clear in the title of our textbook, *Science and Health with Key to the Scriptures*, by Mary Baker Eddy. Science and health. If we truly have Science, we have health. They go together; they can't be separated. You really cannot have Science without having health. As you establish Science in your life, you establish health in your life, and this by divine law and authority. The one establishes the other. See that you really have Science, and it takes care of your health. Your functions, your sight, your hearing, your supply, your happiness, are all intact in the Science of Being. Then have Science, and you have them. You cannot have Science and be without them. Nothing which God gives can ever fail or weaken. Your sight, your hearing, for instance, are being constantly replenished by Him, and His mercies are "new every morning" — every instant. Indeed, your sight and hearing and health and happiness are of and because of His mercy. They just keep right on coming out of heaven to you because of their inexhaustible source and unending vitality. You are composed of mental faculties, and they are always established, for they, like all creation, express the power of an endless life. The power and capacity of your spiritual faculties can never lessen for they are in Science, intact forever.

The entire universe is established also in Science and health. In the sight of Science, of God understood, birth and death for man or for anything that lives, are as unreal as the imaginary equator line. That equator line doesn't separate anything. If we believed it to be a barrier, doubtless we would know nothing that goes on in the southern hemisphere, but we know that line has no substance, and so it hides nothing. So the supposed lines of birth and death do not exist to divine Mind, and they hide nothing that lives and is. Man and the universe exist as one imperishable identity expressing God. And right now we must stand in Science and know the nothingness of the barriers of belief, and enjoy the foreverness and the truth of the real universe. The universe is environment for man — individual man has his place in it. Without real tree, ocean, mountain, sky, blossom, sunrise, cloud, bird, and the little brother we call "creature," life would be blank indeed. It is all included in the power of an endless life, and all stand intact for our discovery and enjoyment, in Science and in health.

There is no such phenomenon in God's universe as a drooping, failing, lacking person, tree, flower, or creature. As God sees His own, it is always in the power of an endless life, and this power

38

forever sustains, invigorates, vivifies all existence and holds this existence at the zenith, the peak, the meridian, of strength, joy, beauty and divine order — in Science and in health. And as we see as God sees, this is all our sure inheritance. In "Pond and Purpose," found in *Miscellaneous Writings*, Mrs. Eddy writes, "What but divine Science can interpret man's eternal existence, God's All-ness, and the scientific indestructibility of the universe."

Recently I heard a good Christian Scientist tell an experience which was amusing, and out of it comes something very lovely for us all to think about. She told of a man who was traveling and having very miserable food served to him time after time, and finally he comforted himself by saying a grace after this fashion, "Father, I thank thee for this as Thou seest it."

Well, why can't that be applied to every trying, discordant situation or experience. "Father, I thank thee for this as Thou seest it." Then we are truly lifting our eyes to God and praising Him for things as they are, for all the good of the universe. To thank Him for this as He sees it — is an "acknowledgment of the perfection of the infinite Unseen," and Mrs. Eddy tells us this "confers a power nothing else can." (*Unity of Good*)

# YOUR DIVINE IDENTITY
## Association Address of 1929

The Bible says that upon a certain occasion when the disciples were together, "The power of the Lord was present to heal them." That power has not changed, nor gone away. Disciples are together again today — here — in His name. So we may justly hope and claim that this power of the Lord is here with us, present to heal us.

If the power of the Lord is present to heal us, it is present to teach us. So we may take our eyes off each other this day and lift them to God who is the only Giver, the only Teacher, the only source of light and help.

If there is one Mind only, then there is only one Mind. This Mind is your real Mind, fundamentally, originally, primarily; you are its idea. This one and only Mind is declaring itself as you constantly to constitute you and empower you. It is as much your Mind as if you were speaking it, and it floods you with light and healing. "Closer to you than breathing," Tennyson wrote, "near than hands and feet," for divine Mind holds you as its own beloved — its own beloved through whom it expresses itself. Your divine Mind which needs you for its expression and in which you find all the Life of being that you really have, alone instructs you, feeds you, renews you, gives you light.

Certain fundamental things are connected with the Christian Science movement:

*The singleness of God's revelation of Him-*
*self to this age through Mary Baker Eddy;*

*The completeness of this revelation, which can never have any further addition to it;*

*The indestructibility of the Cause, the one in-spired source on earth which will give out purely, and protect forever from destruction, the rev-elation which we call Christian Science;*

*Loyalty to your own household in support of all Christian Scientists who stand in posts of responsibility, that there may be one working band, that there may be a forward march of Christian Science.*

### Man as Spiritual Idea

We know the Truth. It reveals God as divine Mind, the one and only Mind, everywhere all-powerful, loving tenderly because it is Love, and caring infinitely for all that it has made because it is infinite.

Through the Old Testament, God declares Himself as "I AM THAT I AM." Divine Mind, the producer and maintainer of the infinite universe, is the one consciousness that can say, "I AM." Man is the reflection of the one consciousness that can say, "I AM." Life, Truth, Love has the capacity to say, "I AM," "I AM HERE," "I AM ALL." Therefore, error cannot say, "I am," "I am here," "I am all," "I am matter," "I am sick or poor or discour-aged." There is only one infinite, impregnable consciousness em-bracing all its ideas in infinite safety.

To understand Life and prove its activity as the spiritual idea is to demonstrate Christian Science.

God is divine Mind, expressing Himself through ideas. All identity, all being, all eternal individuality, whether man or the uni-verse, all that lives and knows it lives, is a spiritual idea.

41

God's ideas, "moving in the harmony of Science" constitute creation. So God's world, of which you are forever a living
part, is a world of spiritual identities. You, spiritual man, are the
immediate object of God's understanding. Mrs. Eddy writes, "Jesus
unveiled the Christ, the spiritual idea of divine Love." This is, of
course, synonymous with unveiling the perfect man; but Mrs. Eddy
specifically uses the term "spiritual idea" to depict the saving aspect of the Christ in relation to the human.

Then Mrs. Eddy uses the term "spiritual idea" with a somewhat different shade of meaning when she writes in *Miscellaneous Writings*, "It is more than a loved person present; it is the
spiritual idea which lights your path." And again, "God gives you
His spiritual ideas, and in turn they give you daily supplies." This
reads as if you, man, are individual spiritual idea, and also that God
sends spiritual ideas to you to sustain and help you.

Man is spiritual idea compounded and composed of all right
ideas. These right ideas are always flowing from God to man,
compounding themselves into the conscious identity of individual
man, composing him, constituting him, supplying him, maintaining
his forever identity as the divine image and likeness, the beloved
son. We might also say that man is compounded of angels. Thus,
we see the way in which Mrs. Eddy used the term "spiritual idea"
— for the entire creation, spiritual man and universe and for the
activity of the Christ Mind, in its saving aspect to human sense, and
as the specific spiritual idea, or angel of understanding, lighting your
human pathway as in, "He gives you spiritual ideas and they give
you daily supplies."

The words *creation*, *man*, *Christ*, *church*, *body*, as Mrs.
Eddy has used them, are just differing approaches, as human language affords them, to the same thing — the infinite manifestation
of infinite Mind. Basically, they are the same thing because there is
only one thing — God and His reflection. Our salvation depends
upon devoted adherence to spiritual idea and upon fidelity in living it
and expressing it.

### Salvation is Within

Salvation is wholly in the realm of thought. Nothing exists to you that you don't mentally recognize and acknowledge. You never have to deal with something outside of your own consciousness, but with that of which you are conscious — your own understanding and your own false belief.

Jesus' parable of the tares and wheat makes this point. The enemy does only one thing — he sows tares among the wheat and then he goes away. He simply sows tares-thinking with wheat-thinking. He declares it is a field of both wheat and tares, and he goes out of sight until Christian Science uncovers him as aggressive mental suggestion. Before you get through with this enemy, you deal with him directly as aggressive mental suggestion, but only and always meeting him as your belief of it. Where is the change to go on? You have no place to work in outside of your own field of thought. The only enemy with which you can have contact is your own belief of evil. So, instead of something outside of your thinking that you have to battle with, stop believing there is an enemy who sowed something and went his way, for God is All-in-all. Then you abandon false mental positions and come into eternally true mental positions, and this is salvation.

You exchange the mind of self, of the flesh, for activity of the spiritual idea; so you exchange trouble and suffering for the security and peace of reality. And you do it just as fast, and it takes you just as far as your measure of activity in the spiritual idea determines. The Christian standardizes his thinking, his acting, by the living example of Christ Jesus and by the revelation of Christian Science. The more actively we think and act in the terms of the spiritual idea, the more rapidly and thoroughly mistaken mental positions are going to leave us. We expect Christian Scientists to live their Christian Science and to think in its terms.

Holding to standardized right thinking, you can drink deeply and constantly at the fount of spiritual ideas open to you by Christian Science. So drinking pure streams of Truth and Life and Love will purify and transform your thoughts; and with your thoughts so purified, your external world will change. The activity of the spiritual idea brings life-giving currents to you, and your body changes, your business changes. All is purified, cleansed, enlarged, set free, as the activity of the spiritual idea works its lovely work with you.

The whole process of regeneration is to change what you think! So watch what you think. You get what you think. And you can always be refusing to think physical sense testimony, and be drinking the water of life, the spiritual idea. The Shunammite woman of the Scriptures fixed her hope in the spiritual facts and did not waiver. She adhered to the spiritual fact, "It is well." She stood with the living spiritual idea and admitted nothing else.

We have said that disease is a wrong way of thinking about yourself, a false mode of thinking. Recognizing that the activity of the spiritual idea is the right mental position, then all belief that life and experience is material is a mistaken mental position. Sin is a false mental position. Disease is a false mental position. Death is a false mental position. The belief that there is matter, is a false mental position, and that is all there is to it. There isn't any substance in matter. Substance is not material. Matter is nothing but a false mental position. And a mental position can be changed. That is how Christian Science heals. It does away with the false mental position and reveals the true one, and things change!

Existence is something entirely different from matter, sin, sickness, and death. Existence is something that is immortal, imperishable being, wholly spiritual. It is Mind and its ideas moving in the heaven of their own celestial harmony.

### Spiritual Ideas Bring Healing

In the work of Christian Science healing, you haven't any matter to cure, to get rid of, or to do anything to. You have only to abandon a false mental position yourself, and help others to abandon it. The activity of the spiritual idea wakens thought from dreaming disease. Sickness is a dream within the dream of life in matter. The dream dreams that body is material, then dreams that disease can be imposed upon the dream body. You first begin to lessen the supposed control of error upon that dream body by rescuing it from the more vicious forms of belief in sin, disease, accident, etc. This freer sense about body comes according to your fidelity to the spiritual idea; and as you gain a delivered sense of body, you learn through Truth that dreams do no governing, and that they can be laid aside for the spiritual idea.

What is the truth about body? Body is the spiritual idea, and the spiritual idea is body. Disease never touches body. Disease appears in the mental realm as belief, and says it can cast a shadow on the body. Whether that shadow is cast on your own personal belief or the general belief, it is erased by a mental change. Disease has no location in body, not even in the human sense of body.

God is Soul. His entire creation is body. Body just means expression, manifestation, emanation, reflection, embodiment of Mind through its ideas. An assemblage of right ideas constitutes man's identity — wholly unorganized because it is reflection. There are no material organs, and no spiritual organs. The spiritual is all idea, reflection. Man is not 'organized.' Body is not 'organized.' There is no matter. Recognize, exalt and stand with body as God knows it — divine idea, individual man, functioning in spiritual integrity in every last particular that pertains to his being. Body is holy and perfect, for perfect man is body.

In a trade journal it was printed, "In a fog there seems to be nothing but ourselves, but when the sun breaks through we see things in their proper relations." This describes the fog of mortal mind. In temptation or suffering, there seems to be nothing but yourself; that little center of yourself around which cluster your aches and pains, troubles, sorrows, fears of all you can see. But cling to spiritual ideas until such activity, such prayers, have displaced the fog of the mistaken mental viewpoint, and the whole landscape of God's true universe, sunlit in divine Love, becomes clear to us; and our humble place in it, rightly related to all the rest of it, is found. And that is heaven. Under the cloud, it may look pretty black and dark, but standing on some peak and looking down on it, you see it filled with silver light, luminous and beautiful in the sunshine. The spiritual idea, we have learned, is not something to be brought to pass. It is always something here to be awakened to, acknowledged, lived, proved. You run into it as a strong tower. You let it unfold your safety, holiness, and health to you.

The steadfast refusal to mentally entertain disease, because of God's allness, destroys it. The activity of the spiritual idea is Christian Science treatment, and Christian Science treatment is the action of the spiritual idea through faithful prayer. To bring this clear-cut, clearly-recognized healing to the world, we must come so close to God in daily thinking that such healing simply pours through a purified, sanctified life. And in all this healing you are not arguing to down something that exists, but awakening yourself from the dream that something other than God exists, from a mistaken mental position.

Disease will never be removed from human life until the mental sense of it is destroyed. Nothing will ever be removed from you except as the mental sense is removed.

Does a Christian Scientist believe that now, here, he has something this time that Christian Science cannot heal? Then he takes a position of great conceit, that you or I as tiny little mortals, could get up something powerful enough to resist omnipotence and infinity. It is a position of egotism and conceit. A world belief that evil can resist the infinity of the Creator who maintains all creation, is the vain boast of world egotism. One real look into infinity surely must silence the vain boasting of "incurable disease."

Our obedient use of what we have of Truth is the open door through which divine Love pours more and more understanding upon us. Christian Science treatment is the activity of the spiritual idea silencing aggressive mental suggestion. Treatment is allowing "nothing but His likeness to abide in your thought." Treatment is letting "neither fear nor doubt overshadow your clear sense and calm trust." Treatment must know three things: the allness of God, the perfection of man, and the nothingness of error.

Matter is not substance. It is a mistaken mental position. Treatment is drawing closer to God in humble prayer, ruling out your own false sense of God and man, exalting the spiritual idea, arguing for the perfection of being, flooding out false pictures with the allness of God realized.

Christian Scientists sometimes satisfy their own thought by "handling" something they think they see needs to be handled, and this results in a relieved belief all around, because the practitioner's thought is satisfied. A complete treatment should not be only that; it should be the scientific destruction of the false claim through the activity of the spiritual idea. That must accompany the handling of any error, else not much has been done except an exchange of belief in the realm of belief. Look to it that your realization of Spirit as supreme is so exalted that the mesmerism of the matter dream is actually broken by the spiritual activity of your treatment. Our own arguments for Truth are good; but let them get you into conscious unity with God as soon as possible.

Too much arguing and handling in daily repetition can get to be rote or formula, and interfere with spontaneity. The constant sense of handling this or that too frequently fixes this or that in your thought. Take time off to enjoy God and His creation. Christian Scientists must not "jell" in what they call their work. They must stay fluid for spiritual activity to change, guide, instruct, and lead them. Let the spontaneity of Soul outline your treatment, awaken you to spiritual ideas, guide you to what you are to see and then unsee.

The form of your treatment should vary with angel guidance. The whole of your work is that error must not be handled as something that you battle with, but as a nothingness that you your-self awaken from — a mistaken mental position that you abandon.

Animal magnetism is the sum total of the world's evil. It is just the universal mistaken mental position about existence. One of your basic points is to let it die for lack of witness. Let it die for lack of witness, after you have been spiritually keen enough to detect it. Abandon your own belief that evil is power.

True Christian Scientists must be alert to the subtleties of evil, and especially does the good and harmless human person have to be educated out of his dumbness, his actual dumbness, concern-ing the deviltry of evil; but the activity of the spiritual idea will keep you all the while illumined with the truth of the nothingness of the very evil you have to face. The well-balanced Christian Scientist, while seeing and then unseeing animal magnetism thoroughly and consistently, will at the same time so uplift the goodness of God and the power of Truth in every thought he thinks and in every word he says, that no one can leave his presence with an increased fear of evil. Everyone should leave his presence with a diminished fear of evil, an easier trust in good.

The claim of evil is just the mist of evil tying to hide God from us. The mist is aggressive; yes, that is its nature; but that does not mean that it has any power. It is truly at enmity with Christ, and would, if it could, stop Christian healing. This aggression can really all be named under the one head — the world's hatred of Truth.

A sample treatment on the question of handling error broadly and as a whole would be as follows:

Divine Mind is everywhere present, all powerful, all divine, filling all consciousness, endowing all its ideas with its own pres-ence and power reflected. Divine Mind is upbearing all, creating on pinions of light; and in its universe, man was never born into any reality of matter, but has always remained, is now, and ever will be, the beloved spiritual image and likeness of an all-tender Father-Mother, Love.

Therefore, this being true, what is called animal magnetism, the mist that went up from the earth, is without form and void. If void, it is vacuity, nothingness, without power or presence. And it is without form; it cannot take the shape of anything.

Being without form, animal magnetism cannot take the shape of man, or church, or government, or politics, or education. It cannot take the shape of a candidate, a teacher, a writer, a preacher. It cannot take the shape of theology, medicine, superstition, occultism, aroused hatred of the Christ, or hatred and destruction of all that is good. It is without form and void.

Animal magnetism cannot take the shape of business, home relationship, work, employment or unemployment; cannot take the shape of lack of income or supply, because business, home, employment, relationship, supply, are all safe in God as spiritual ideas knowing no taint of matter; all are safe in divine Mind which knows all there is to be known about them, and keeps that one's true mental position about them. Animal magnetism cannot take the shape of man, woman, child, creation, misunderstanding, ambitious candidate electioneering, unbrotherliness in any way, for it is without form and void. It cannot take the shape of organized or unorganized enmity towards Christian Science. Animal magnetism has no faculties, no perception, or powers of discernment; those all belong to Mind. It has no claim to beauty, intelligence, affection, goodness; those all belong to Soul. It cannot take the shape of pleasure or satisfaction; that is all found in Spirit. It cannot claim to be facts, for facts all belong to Truth.

Animal magnetism has no capacity to discern man or make conditions for him, cannot locate man or the universe. Animal magnetism has no capacity to formulate, prophesy, entangle, confuse, darken, because it is without form and is void. The GREAT I AM has the only capacity to say "I AM." Animal magnetism cannot take the shape of unyielding patients or burdened practitioners, for it cannot call itself sick or burdened persons; man is free-born, and the activity of the spiritual idea, denying all life or identity to animal magnetism, releases thought not only to enjoy creation as it is, but also to have an improved belief of life, health, happiness, right here and now to human sense.

Whatever in your thinking hides your God-like brother from you, must go from your own thought before you can get fully into heaven. Disease is nonexistent, never present, nowhere, because God fills all space, all consciousness.

Every inch of consciousness has to be cleansed of error, that Truth may consciously possess it. The whole point is never to descend into the personal. Be as concrete and as specific as you like in dealing with any phase of error, but never see it as personal. To stand, refusing to let mortal mind tell you anything about yourself or anybody or anything except the absolute Truth of perfection, takes heaven-borne and heaven-sustained courage.

To be wise enough to ask God for wisdom is the greatest wisdom. The great wisdom is not to get involved in error, to keep detached, and so to keep from being handled by it. The whole of wisdom lies in hearing the voice of God and then obeying it.

A Christian Scientist can be extremely ill and yet be getting well all the time. Why is this so? Because he knows how to let divine Mind keep renewing him in the face of the claim. Divine Mind in action, as spiritual idea, constitutes you, and is a constant law of recovery to you, no matter what the senses are saying. Keeping the spiritual idea active gives you continual recuperation, and you can never be overtaxed if you are faithful. God is not the author of confusion, and we must prove it by our reflected peace intelligence, and love.

The human mind is one great longing, or great question. God is our infinite ever-present Mind. Reflect Him, and you have your infinite all. You reflect your final triumphant rest in God — not in the future, but now. And what you reflect is the activity of the spiritual idea which bestows itself upon your human need, amplifying and extending your whole being with capacity, vitality, health, and abundance of good in all ways.

And so at all times gather up your human needs and bring

them under the shining tents of the divine protection of Love. Under Love's sheltering canopy, you find your need dissolving in ever-present supply of all that constitutes your life and being. In the precious secret place of the Most High, your need disappears in fulfillment.

# THE UNSEEN EMBODIMENT
## Association Address

In *Science and Health with Key to the Scriptures*, Mary Baker Eddy, says, "The good you do and embody gives you the only power obtainable." We may know, then, that goodness is man, and that the spiritual identity of goodness is the only body man has. There are no material organs. There are no spiritual organs, as Spirit does not organize, it reflects. It is embodiment, spiritual identity, and it is wholly good.

God expresses Himself in man and the universe, and that expression, manifestation, impartation, reflection, is the one indivisible body — which is generic man. Individual specific man has his place in this one indivisible embodiment called generic man as the ray of sunlight has its place in the indivisible body of sunlight.

Man is not someone who has a body. Man himself is body, or the embodiment, of right ideas. Man is not a spiritual idea with a body, but the spiritual idea, identity, is body. Mortal belief says, "I will organize him into a little individual mind and a little personal body." That is the lie about man. Organization is the lie. Spiritual man, or any body, is unorganized. Reflection cannot be organized any more than sunlight can be organized. Reflection is being.

The infinite manifestation is generic man, and so individual man is the embodiment of right ideas in individual spiritual identity. The lie says that this idea is organized into matter. It is not. And remember not to make the mistake of thinking the original of the lie could be spiritual organs. It is all reflection, individually expressed. The knowledge of God, individually expressed, is the real man. In *Science and Health* we read, "Organization and time have nothing to do with life." We know that the functioning or activity of the real man is wholly a matter of reflection — all spiritual, the embodiment of right ideas. That is the truth about which a so-called mortal body is a lie. What it is, we do not see yet; but when we awake in His likeness, we shall be satisfied. And the unseen embodiment is manifested now in more goodness and health in daily life, and in what humans see as a better body.

## The Unseen

"As seeing Him who is invisible." So the writer of the Book of Hebrews defined the outlook of the early Christians. That same outlook is defined by the author of the Christian Science text-book in this age — the later Christians. Mrs. Eddy writes, "The heavens and earth to one human consciousness, that consciousness which God bestows, are spiritual, while to another, the unillumined human mind, the vision is material." The same heavens and the same earth. There is only one. To the unillumined mind, it is material. To the consciousness which God bestows, it is spiritual. We can say, then, that the Christian Scientist is the illumined mind which is beginning to see and live in "Him who is invisible" to unillumined materiality.

As students of Christian Science, we are much in the position of Elisha's servant as related in II Kings: "An host compassed the city" and Elisha prayed that the eyes of his servant be opened. They were, and he then became aware of the greater host of helpers, symbolized to him as the mountain full of horses and chariots of fire round about Elisha. Not scattered everywhere, please note, but round about Elisha, who was lifting his thought to companion with them; whose faith really summoned them, and whose spiritual sight beheld them.

Here was a specific spiritual experience in which prayer and trust revealed the Unseen so that it became seen. Then the seen vision of the hitherto Unseen put to flight fear and doubt, and good prevailed.

Our eyes are opened when we see Christian Science to be revealed Truth. As we hold them open by faith and prayer, and what we call treatment, we become aware of the angels of the Unseen, we cling to them, and realize their work with us, and for us, in the power of spiritual ideas. Spiritual faith, clinging to spiritual power, motivates and empowers every Christian Science treatment. The entire life of a Christian Scientist is based upon the presence, power and guidance of the Unseen. Thought closed to the seen materiality of the physical senses, and open to the vision of Spirit, constitutes, and is, the state of mind called a genuine Christian Scientist.

What but open spiritual vision could have saved Paul and his fellows from shipwreck, opened prison doors for Peter, and kept the face of Stephen like that of an angel while he was being stoned to death? Would a personal God see Peter's plight and say, "There is Peter in jail. I like him. He is working for me, and I'll get him out because he prayed to me?" Not at all. Peter's spiritual vision saw the true nature of God and saw that the dream of hatred's bolts had no resistance to the will of God. Peter's own seeing of the Unseen summoned the angels, and brought divine power to bear upon his dilemma, and the circumstances changed.

What sustained the ancient prophets and early Christians through affliction? Was it not the eye of faith which "endures as seeing Him who is invisible"? Through faith they saw spiritual reality displace material claims, saw healing and the dead raised to life.

They saw through the eyes of faith, and then saw the power of their seeing work out for good. That is what the genuine Christian Scientist is about today. The power of seeing is a reflected power, of course, since all power belongs to God. The reflected power which comes of seeing and knowing Him who is invisible is the healing agent. The Revelator of Truth in this age, Mary Baker Eddy, wrote in *Unity of Good*, "Certain self-proved propositions pour into my waiting thought in connection with these experiences;

and here is one such conviction; that an acknowledgment of the perfection of the infinite Unseen confers a power nothing else can." Being a Christian Scientist means keeping the spiritual gaze fixed upon spiritual sense, translating the perfection of the Unseen into the seen and recognizing its healing presence, which redeems the woes of mankind.

It is the effort of animal magnetism at all times to shut out spiritual vision. It is, contrariwise, the effort of the Christian Scientist to pray for spiritual vision, to keep it open through more prayer, to defend it against further attacks by the seen, and to recognize its healing presence which redeems further prayer, and also to enlarge its borders by meditating upon the deep things of God. "Faith should enlarge its borders," the textbook tells us. It is no wonder that modern thought is atheistic. Through physical senses, you learn nothing about God. Matter is all that can be heard, seen, felt, tasted, smelled by the physical senses. Physical sense is an unbeliever in anything spiritual. It cannot see God. Modern material thought is wholly godless. Mrs. Eddy notes in the textbook that "God is not seen by the material sense," but writes, conversely, "Through spiritual sense you can discern the heart of divinity." "Spiritual sense," she tells us, "is a conscious, constant capacity to understand God."

A hunger for the pure and the good which outweighs every material attraction, is the open road to spiritual sense. There spiritual sense is awakened and operative; there is God known; and that awakening, even in its small beginning, unveils the infinite, links thought to God, plants the outlook in the eternal. It empowers the present experience with the victories of good to the extent that spiritual understanding appears, acts, and works out blessings. Such an awakening produces a Christian Scientist and starts him on his task of proving the divine Unseen to be here as power, presence and savior.

It is as if we become a watered garden with the source of the spring unseen. Parched gardens may lie all about us, but our "acknowledgment of the perfection of the infinite Unseen" will keep our garden fresh and green and flowering, and in time bring its unseen living waters to all the gardens which thirst for them.

Let us look at the Unseen as Christian Science unveils it, in the subject of God, man, Christ, body, supply, salvation. Fundamentally the outlook of the Christian Scientist differs from that of everyone else on earth. Those who see being as matter, as evil and destruction, see God, man, and salvation through a glass darkly. The Christian Scientist accepts revelation about these great subjects, strips his thought of false viewpoints, sees creation from a spiritual viewpoint; and then, if he applies properly what he sees, he is as an archangel. His understanding is a flaming sword to sever error from thought and to win the world to Christ.

The renowned physicist Dr. A. Michelson has said that unflagging pursuit of absolute accuracy was the key to his wonderful scientific researches. The world is indeed fortunate that Mrs. Eddy was inspired to unflagging pursuit of "absolute accuracy" in spiritual things. With absolute accuracy we can prove the actual, eternal Truth of being in our daily lives.

Think of it: The law which governs the stars in their courses can govern the least detail of our lives, mind, body, when we accept and obey these laws and what Christian Science is revealing to us. Let us sum up what it reveals to us. First, the hitherto unseen God as spiritual understanding reveals Him — Divine Mind, holding the infinity of the universe within His own self-containment, seeing in all of this creation never-ending, never-changing perfection. There is His own magnitude, might, glory, dominion, holiness, and beauty reflected in the boundless expression of Himself upon the face of all creation, enclosed within His own infinity. As divine Principle, God is both source and boundless circumference, cause and effect, the allness, the origin and the entire completeness of all that exists.

God is Truth, never altering His unending nature and characteristics. God is Spirit, knowing no substance save pure Mind which can never break down nor decay. God is Soul, alive with the genius of creative enjoyment, inspiration and appreciation. God as Soul, endows all creation with inspirational initiative and capacity to enjoy everything lovely. God as Soul makes all existence one of inspiration and bliss.

God is Life, not just a God who is alive, making living things, but Life itself, characterizing all creation as quality and condition. God is Love, with the joy of constantly making happy and safe and right everything within the range of His all-encompassing, bestowing, sheltering, tender compassion. Looking through the lens of Christian Science, these divine hues of Deity appear.

As earlier noted, the textbook says, "Man is the expression of God's being." Man is then the expression of all this glory, beauty, joy — the indestructibility of infinite Mind. God and man are as bound together as Mind and idea can be. But man is not God, any more than a thought of yours, to use a human parallel, is your mind. God and man are cause and effect. God is Mind, and man is the result of the action of Mind. One in essence, but distinct as cause and effect. Again, as noted earlier, we read from our textbook that "Infinite Mind can never be in man, but is reflected by man," and "Man is not God, but like a ray of light that comes from the sun, man, the outcome of God, reflects God."

When God looks into the mirror of spiritual understanding or divine Science, what does He see? He sees Himself reflected, and that reflection constitutes man and the universe. God reflects Himself to Himself, and this reflection constitutes man. Man is the reflection. Man is not outside of divine Mind, but expressed within divine Mind. Man is as limitless as God is limitless: "Whatever is possible to God is possible to man as God's reflection." We can then say that man is without limits, because God is without limits. No human words could better express the height, breadth and depth of reflected infinity, which constitutes man as "the infinite idea forever developing itself." Humans may stagger at the thought of " . . . rising higher and higher from a boundless basis," but ponder this, and infinity will become more real to you. In *Miscellaneous Writings*, Mrs. Eddy states that man "cannot get out of the focal distance of infinity." This is the man whom God sees, but which the physical senses can never see.

Christian Science reveals this wonder and glory to you, and sets about proving this boundless reflected consciousness in you. Learn to identify yourself always as reality, as real man.

### The Hitherto Unseen Christ

To understand the unseen Christ, we must know something of the words *reflection* and *impartation*. Christ is the sum total of the full reflection of divine Mind, and in this sense it is synonymous with generic man. God and Christ are Principle and idea, Cause and effect, Soul and body, infinite Mind and its infinite manifestation, Father-Mother and the beloved Son. Christ is the impartation of God. Impartation means to bestow, to communicate the knowledge of. Divine Mind bestows Himself upon His universe and communicates the knowledge of Himself to and through His idea, because man is the knowledge of God. Divine Mind is always imparting itself, not through subdivision, not through minds many, but by the one indivisible expression of Himself.

All reflection as a whole — the complete sum total of reflection — constitutes the Christ as generic man; such as the whole body of sunlight reflected undivided — one Light, one Christ. Then the individual understanding of God, the individual man, the real you or me, is like the individual ray of light imparted from the source and reflecting the whole light. God is individual, and so His reflection must express individuality. As a ray of light would not be light unless it expressed warmth and light from its source, so man must reflect the whole nature of the source from which he comes. The unseen Christ saves by Christianizing the personal life. Any amount of talking about the sun would not revive anything. The warmth and light itself must come to make things live and grow. So the warmth and light of Christliness must be lived in order to experience salvation.

## *Salvation*

Not one bit of salvation is evident until the infinite Unseen begins to take the place of the physically seen — until our seeing chariots of fire on the mountain empowers faith to rout sin and fear. We never forget that those spiritually aware of God through the ages have had something of God to sustain them. As salvation operates in Christian Science, it can be summed up in one word, *correction*. There is no Christ to you or me, theorize as we may, except as today's thought is Christianized. The word *Christ* connotes the saving aspect of God's love, and that saving is correction by absolute spiritual accuracy. Thus, the unseen Christ becomes seen in a corrected life, and that is the only way it can be seen. The seeing comes right along with purifying; and purifying increases with the seeing.

Salvation turns our thought to Christian Science treatment, and Christian Science treatment is the instrument of salvation. In considering treatment, we see that it does two things: It reveals the true nature of God, and uncovers the untrue nature of animal magnetism. Salvation, as an active corrective, must unmask Satan — put him out of business. And Mrs. Eddy's great and definite service to the race was her perception that all materiality, instead of being God-fathered and God-permitted, was an illusive counterfeit or falsity, having no real existence in the sight of God. We must recognize that just as God's nature has been unseen by the material senses, so the claims of animal magnetism have been hidden to them, unseen by them. Just as Christian Science reveals the hitherto unseen God, so it reveals and exposes the hitherto unseen Satan.

Salvation means thought set free from believing the animal magnetic lie. It is the sense of good which the material senses see not. It takes dedicated effort to understand this. The dulled and deceived physical senses neither see God as He is, nor Satan as he claims to be. Mrs. Eddy reduced evil to its native nothingness — no thing — and named it animal magnetism. It is animal in nature and propensity; magnetic in its methods — the entire material round of human birth, development, decay and death.

A Christian Scientist enjoys reducing animal magnetism to nothingness in consciousness, through knowing the allness of God. He enjoys facing animal magnetism, dealing with it, robbing it of all claims to place, plan, nature, law, action or power to operate or to be. "Matter is hell," one of the early teachers said, "and Christian Science treatment is the shortest way out of it." One must rise up out of it and get out and stay out by facing its claims, by bringing heaven to bear upon them. It is not wise to believe that hell has power and position, for the Christian Scientist is to be persuaded of the allness of God, and the total unreality of evil. From this vantage point, uncover and denounce and annul the claims of animal magnetism as they come to light through the advancing interest and understanding of Truth's ability to render them powerless.

The so-called world of crookedness and sin is only a voice saying man is not spiritual. It has no substance. This voice is quenched and corrected by Christian Science treatment. Handling error is much like using a broom. You sweep a room, not because you want contact with the dirt, but because you want to clean your room.

In the same way, it is necessary to use the broom of argument against the particular bit of dust that needs sweeping out of our thinking. And if we are alert, we are glad to do the work, play the game, use the broom. We neither ignore animal magnetism, nor blow the breath of life into it by believing it to be real or having power. We disarm it. To ignore it is to fail in your work. God guides you to proper treatment of it as you turn to Him for guidance. And you come to see that in all the stretches of eternity there is no such thing as animal magnetism.

God's perfect creation has never been reversed. When you pray the prayer that handles animal magnetism, do a thorough job. Don't just fuss over someone's temper, or jealousy in your circle of persons and events; don't go about with mysterious whisperings of Roman Catholicism and malpractice, which whispers are sometimes very unintelligent; don't hunt for somebody's thinking as the cause of your trouble; don't let any organized system of teaching, whether political, religious, or medical, stand out as your specialty. But go back of personal or institutional systems to the one lying voice which would claim a mind apart from God. Turn off the whole fountain. We may brush off the drops, but unless we turn off the whole fountain, the drops will keep coming.

To rid the race of belief in evil, you need to do more than deal with the evil which you see. Take your denial back to the original serpent, back to the lying voice which would reverse God and His creation. And so, for handling error specifically, take your denial back to the ancient magic of the Chaldees, that hoary black art wherein mortal mind achieves the most subtle manipulation of itself, and which has come down through the ages into the occult teaching of the present day Eastern Indian magic, and in the various cultivations of occultism in the darkest of earth's mentalities.

In one big sweep deny any past, present, or future to such subtleties. Our treatment should be just as broad and thorough as our textbook. It is understood that this old Eastern magic boasts of using modern Jesuitism as a cat's paw — that is, it can set the nations at variance and even produce dissension and war at will, by its mental means. Then why should our treatment not be broad enough to work out deliverance from this ancient lie — animal magnetism? Christian Science has come to deliver the race, its entire routine and destiny, from every entanglement of evil laws, and so our treatments must compass the sum total of the false claims. Christian Science gives us a true education about the false claim of evil. We do not need to delve into error, hunt around for it — mentally associate with it — but we do have to receive willingly the education and uncovering which Christian Science gives about it. We have to be teachable about the general nature of error, as

61

well as of Truth. Unseeing the whole thing, turning off the whole fountain, we can protect our governments, peace councils, everything, from maliciously superinduced misunderstandings. We can pray the prayer which protects right issues, and which keeps our wise and good statesmen clear in thought and living on to express their ideals.

What we need in our work is to get unlocalized, away from petty personal problems into the one great issue of deliverance for the whole human family. Someone said: "To personalize is to problemize; to universalize is to spiritualize." We cannot personalize. We must universalize. Get upon the mountain top. Look down from spiritual heights. Identify yourself always with God and the real man. Stand as Michael and Gabriel combined, to bring heaven to bear upon the human problem. "Never let thought bump the earth." Keep it up in inspiration and understanding and reality. "People sad and bad or glad, people wild or tame, looked at from a mountain top seem about the same."

Our work is not with each other, but to correct our own thinking about each other. We stay at home mentally and correct our own thought about everything. When we criticize unkindly, right there we weaken our own spiritual strength. When we gossip, we descend from the height. We soil our own high thought every time we do it. Looking at existence through personal sense, dims our light. Keep your thought soaring. Harry Emerson Fosdick, an eminent theologian, says: "Christianity is retarded not so much by the antagonism of the non-believer, as by the pettiness of the believers. Refuse to be disturbed by petty things. This is the secret of poise."

In connection with purification, we all need what Mrs. Eddy said in a letter: "The distemper of pride is more dangerous than small-pox. It is the ugliest pox in the land. Its postules leave the ugliest scars. How long do place and power in human thought last? Hardly over night. Your position in spiritual demonstration is the only position you have or ever can have. It may call upon you to serve in certain ways, but that is only secondary. Your spiritual position in dissolving Satan and exalting the Christ is the only position you have. That maintains itself, whether mortal mind recognizes it or not. It can always be your crown and joy. Exalt God and denounce evil. Your footing in Spirit is all there is to you." In connection with this thought Mrs. Eddy writes in *Pulpit and Press*, "Popularity, self-aggrandizement, aught that can darken in any degree our spirituality, must be set aside. Only what feeds and fills the sentiment with unworldliness, can give peace and good will toward men." You have to detect error.

We do see something of the infinite Unseen. Christian Science has unveiled it to us. The next step is to have faith in what we see and to have faith in the power of our seeing. We do not live in matter — we live in Spirit. If we live in Spirit, there is no sin, disease, age, nor death, for there is no time or space in Spirit, and no matter to have any age. I have been told that Mrs. Eddy once said, "Never wait for that which can never come. Neither age nor death can come to man. They cannot take lodgement with the spiritual idea, any more than darkness can find footing in light."

We do not need any human strength to overcome evil. We have confidence in the power of our seeing the infinite. We do what the Book of Jude says that Michael the archangel did, when contending with the devil. He said: "The Lord rebuke thee." When we call upon the great Unseen, identify with it and strive to realize its allness, we set in motion the spiritual currents which move upon the waters of mortal mind and purify them. Everything good in Truth is everywhere all the time. Your health is wherever you are. It can never leave you nor can you ever leave it. Your sight, hearing, all the faculties of perception, are in their fullness all the time. You possess them by reflection. Guard your possession by knowing their indestructibility, their eternality.

Your sight and hearing are you, a component part of you. You reflect your faith, your guidance, and when and how to rest in the infinite Unseen. You reflect the strength to stay on the mountain top of the one Mind; the initiative to open opportunities, the intuition to see the chariots of fire. You reflect faith and understanding to summon angels as could your Master; and you reflect the power of the Unseen, and with it the intelligence to trust that power and see it as God's work.

The claims of animal magnetism cannot prevent your demonstration of Christian Science, world without end. Every right prayer, every treatment keeps the spiritual vision open to all the glory of God. We read in *Science and Health*, "To material sense, this divine universe is dim and distant, grey in the somber hues of twilight, but anon the veil is lifted, and the scene shifts into light." Christian Science lifts the veil and the Unseen becomes the Seen.

## *Unlabored Motion*

We need more and more the unlabored motion, spontaneity, quick and sure faith. There should be a natural, satisfying inflow of good from the unseen source of good all the time. As Longfellow beautifully puts it: "Streams rise because God at our fountain far off has been raining." We rise because God at our fountain right here is raining. Strain and mental labor are not the inflow of God, but the human effort in some way to find it. The labor and the wrestling are with the fear and the limitation which would prevent trust and confidence and resting in the Lord. Argument is used just to subdue our own fear and doubt. Do not take these remarks as meaning that mental argument and labor are not at times necessary. They are. Mental reasoning, mental labor, faithful rejection of evil and acceptance of good, are ways by which we climb the mountain much of the time, the way by which we persuade ourselves of the power of good. We sometimes have to keep a faithful vigil through a long siege, through a night of watching until the day breaks. A lot of our limitation and lack are because we do not keep that vigil long and faithful enough. A large part of our labor is due to our undestroyed fear of and belief in evil as power. We willingly keep the vigil. We wrestle as Jacob did, when we must; but as fearlessness develops, and we know better that the power is all with God, the joy of finding rest with God should be more and more with us. As this sure sense grows, the form of treatment changes.

Sudden inspiration settles many questions for us. That is why there can be no formula for treatment. In treatment we may become too technical, too analytical, too curious about evil. Inspiration, faith, trust, lifts us above these ways that are sometimes called intellectual gymnastics. Harry Emerson Fosdick says we should enjoy and not make a problem of everything. When we make too much of problems, we lose the beauty of life; though to have no problem would be to become a sentimentalist. Then he goes on to say: "Man does not need to understand all the problems of the atmosphere to breathe and enjoy the air."

If you watch your step too closely, it cramps your stride. Stride out in faith and trust. If error says you do not know how to walk with God, walk with Him any way you can. If it says you cannot give a treatment, give it anyway. Pray just anyway you can. Call on the northwest wind which you may not fully understand, but know it is there to blow the fog away. Rise and greet the winds of God in faith and trust, and with a childlike heart, and there won't be any fog. The wind has swept it away.

We talk about mental background. God is the only mental background, but mortal mind claims one that looks like an old-fashioned quilt. An illusive mental reservoir claims to be mind apart from God, claims to furnish mortals with many undesirable suggestions. It is animal magnetism's structure and nature — the unseen evil which Truth uncovers that it may be seen. Every treatment should not only cover the visible cause of the trouble, but also blot out the claim of a subconscious mental reservoir from which visible cause springs. Turn off the fountain.

## *No Condemnation*

An effectual way to give a healing treatment is to realize there is no condemnation. Mortal mind has condemned its false concept of man and creation to sin, sickness, and death, to hate, discord, and woe. As someone has put it, "The false accusers accuse all of us as being animal, when in reality God has made us spiritual."

God's idea knows nothing of accusation. Man stands in the light of God's reflection, perfect, untouched, radiant in goodness, never descending into false belief. The accuser is the only thing that hears the accusation — accusing its own beliefs about itself. The accuser is an illusion having no location, no purpose, no voice, no power, no mind. But to dispose of it intelligently, we need to regard it as one — accuser and condemnation. One voice condemning everybody and everything. It would blight its own false sense of creation. If we really watch our own thought, we are astonished to see how blame and condemnation operate in our own thought against persons and things. God has never condemned man nor any living thing. His law condemns sin to perish. He ordains the whole of creation to freedom.

If you separate error from thought, you detect error; but you do not condemn man; you free man. As our present feeble sense of the infinite glory of man and creation has personal condemnation removed from it, we shall spring into light and joy even now. "No condemnation" of man or the universe is a beautiful treatment.

## *Christian Science Treatment*

Christian Science treatment is the way out of hypnotism into life. It is the activity of Christ dispelling false suggestions. There is no human element in Christian Science treatment, because Christian Science practice is simply the government of God understood and demonstrated. Treatment is God declaring Himself. God gives the treatment; you listen. Treatment brings forward what God wills for man, and puts to flight what man would selfishly will for himself. Christian Science treatment does not pamper self; it does not pad nor strengthen materiality.

Primarily, Christian Science treatment calls man up from material belief into spiritual experiences. It frees from the flesh. Christian Science does not bring health nor success to animality, but strikes animality out of thought. It does not help us to get what we want, but it helps us to want what is right. Only that which is fit for the kingdom of heaven can thrive under Christian Science treatment. Evil withers away. Webster defines treatment as "management; handling; usage." So your daily usage of Truth to destroy error is your treatment of error — your attitude towards preventing evil suggestions from entering your thinking. Your mental work constitutes your treatment. What you do with a thing is your treatment of it. Your treatment puts the claim of evil to flight. And when your conduct, your deportment, combine with your understanding, to correct and spiritualize your life, it goes so far as to heal the sick and sinning; then they have become what Christian Science calls demonstration. The divine Unseen has been brought to bear upon the falsely seen. Again, when you have become that state of prayer, that state of behavior, and exalt God, and abolish evil, your treatment is perpetual, perennial — the inflow of life close to God proving constantly His effectual glory.

Your life has then been like the Holy City — four-square and perfect, a constant intake of divine Love and continuous expenditure of it for others.

A helpful point in treatment is to speak with authority. Who speaks? God Himself. Not you as a mortal. Why not, then, speak with full authority? Jesus did it. Some of the authoritative commands in *Science and Health* are "rise in rebellion"; "banish the belief"; "rule out"; "blot out the images of mortal thought"; "be firm in your understanding."

I think that we have the right to order mortal mind to let go of our health, our homes, our business, our supply, our happiness and all our affairs. It has no discernment to find them anyhow. Then speak with the authority that Mrs. Eddy had in mind when she said in *Unity of Good*, "Jesus demanded a change of consciousness and evidence." He knew from what basis to demand it, by what law and power; and so do we. If you are a good working Christian Scientist, you know almost as much about being as anyone on earth. Think what you know. You know the Truth of being. You know what life is and what it is all about, what salvation is and how to go about it. Why not exalt what you know and speak with authority? Why not, with your Master, demand it?

When we linger in trouble, in fear, we are being somewhat deferential to the devil, a little too polite. In the name of God demand a change of consciousness.

ABOUT THE AUTHOR: Blanche Hersey Hogue, C.S.B., was one of the early workers in the Christian Science movement. She became interested in Christian Science as a young woman. She had begun a musical career as a pianist. But a healing of her mother in Christian Science caused her to give up her career in music and devote her full time to the healing work. She became a member of The Mother Church in July of 1893.

At the time that she became a member of The Mother Church, she also helped organize First Church of Christ, Scientist in Portland, Oregon, and served as its Pastor until Mrs. Eddy ordained the Bible and *Science and Health* as the pastor of all Christian Science Churches. Mrs. Hogue was elected First Reader of that branch church.

Mrs. Hogue was not a student of Mrs. Eddy, but she did earn the degree of C.S.B. in 1899, and was a dedicated practitioner and teacher for over fifty years. She was also elected to a three year term as Second Reader of The Mother church in July of 1914.

Mrs. Hogue contributed many articles to the Christian Science periodicals. In *Miscellany* page 237, Mrs. Eddy mentions Mrs. Hogue in recommending that all Christian Scientists carefully study her article on the *Church Manual* printed in the *Christian Science Sentinel* of September 10, 1910.

For further information regarding Christian Science:
Write:  The Bookmark
Post Office Box 801143
Santa Clarita, CA 91380
Call:  1-800-220-7767
Visit our website:  www. thebookmark.com

For further information regarding Christian Science:
Write:  The Bookmark
             Post Office Box 801143
             Santa Clarita, CA 91380
Call:   1-800-220-7767
Visit our website:  www. thebookmark.com